SOLOMON SPEAKS

SPEAKS

ON
RECONNECTING
YOUR LIFE

ALSO BY DR. ERIC PEARL

The Reconnection: Heal Others, Heal Yourself

Please visit:

Hay House USA: **www.hayhouse.com**®
Hay House Australia: **www.hayhouse.com.au**
Hay House UK: **www.hayhouse.co.uk**
Hay House India: **www.hayhouse.co.in**

SOLOMON SPEAKS
ON
RECONNECTING
YOUR LIFE

Dr. Eric Pearl
and
Frederick Ponzlov

HAY HOUSE, INC.
Carlsbad, California • New York City
London • Sydney • New Delhi

Published in the United States by: Hay House, Inc.: www.hayhouse.com® • **Published in Australia by:** Hay House Australia Pty. Ltd.: www.hayhouse.com.au • **Published in the United Kingdom by:** Hay House UK, Ltd.: www.hayhouse.co.uk • **Published in India by:** Hay House Publishers India: www.hayhouse.co.in

Cover design: Matteo Venturi, Edizioni My Life, Italy, info@mylife.it
Interior design: Pamela Homan

Library of Congress Cataloging-in-Publication Data

Pearl, Eric.
  Solomon speaks on reconnecting your life / Eric Pearl, Frederick Ponzlov.
    pages cm
   ISBN 978-1-4019-4296-0 (hardback) -- ISBN 978-1-4019-4295-3 (tradepaper) 1. Mental healing. 2. Spiritual healing. 3. Mind and body. I. Ponzlov, Frederick. II. Title.
  RZ401. P37 2013
  615.8'528--dc23

                              2013001573

Hardcover ISBN: 978-1-4019-4296-0
Tradepaper ISBN: 978-1-4019-4295-3

1st edition, May 2013

Printed in the United States of America

CONTENTS

PROLOGUE

Eric's Story

Oh my God! I thought, watching my patient, Fred, who was no longer simply lying on his back on the cushioned table in front of me in my office. *No one is going to believe this. Who or what am I in the presence of?*

Fred's eyes were partially closed as they rolled up and back into his skull and began to dart rapidly back and forth underneath his fluttering eyelids. His breathing slowed and became deep. His arms, somewhat extended to the sides, began to move slowly, rhythmically . . . gently up, then down, then up again, as if softly buoyed by an invisible energy field. His lips parted; you could see that his tongue was moving in a manner that was clearly forming speech as air audibly escaped his mouth.

With slight trepidation, I bent forward and brought my ear closer to hear what he had to say . . . yet all I could make out was the sound of his breath as the aspirations attempted in vain to form themselves into words.

I was frozen in place by sheer awe. I knew I was in the presence of something grander than I, or most people—or perhaps anyone at all—had ever experienced.

And yet this was neither the beginning nor the end of something that would move beyond what I could have ever anticipated, something that would soon affect millions of people around the globe.

As I listened carefully to the sound of the air coming from Fred, I *did* finally hear a voice. Not from Fred. It was the voice of my mother saying, *What are you doing?! Get your ear away from the crazy person before he bites it off!* And I started to smile, to laugh inside. It's hard to explain what it's like to be somewhat frightened, in awe, and struck by humor at the same time. . . .

Now, before I continue along this line, can I truthfully say that this came *totally* out of the blue? Well, yes . . . and no. To be more clear, let me back up just a few months from that January day in 1994 to the previous August.

Little did I know that life was about to change for me, and for many people. For the previous 12 years, I had been very happy as a doctor. I had one of the largest and most successful chiropractic practices in Los Angeles, and that was how I thought I would spend my life. But, you see, I went home on a Thursday *thinking* that I was a doctor of chiropractic, and when I came back on the following Monday, I was something else. (Mind you, my parents had always told me that I *was* "something else"—but this probably wasn't what they had in mind.)

It all started on that Thursday night, when I was suddenly awakened by a very bright light. I opened my eyes to see what it was, and it wasn't anything seemingly spiritual or metaphysical: It was just the lamp next to my bed. It had turned itself on. Now I'd had this lamp for over ten years at the time, and it hadn't selected any other occasion to self-illuminate. Yet there it was.

At the same time, it felt as though someone was in my home.

I can't begin to describe what an eerie feeling it is to wake up to the sense that somebody is in your house who hadn't been there when you went to sleep. Let's just say that I got up with a knife, a can of pepper spray, and my Doberman pinscher and went hunting. After a good 20 minutes, I decided that it had to be my imagination and went back to sleep. But on the following Monday, seven of my patients, independently of one another, insisted that they were feeling "people" in the rooms of my office as we worked, just as I had felt people in my home—although they were completely unaware of my experience.

Now, after 12 years of practice and no one having said anything remotely similar to that up until then, you would think that seven people telling me this all in one day would get my attention. But you see, other patients that same day were telling me that they could feel my hands without me actually touching them. Of course I didn't believe them. I told them to lie on the table with their eyes closed as I held my hands inches to feet to yards away from them, yet they could always tell the direction my palms were facing. *Left ankle, right shoulder.* They knew. They could *feel* me . . . or *it.*

As I watched, their facial muscles—tiny muscles in their forehead or around their chin and lips—would move . . . would, more accurately, *ripple.* Muscles that were so small they couldn't be moved intentionally. Lips would part; tongues would move. Eyes would rapidly dart back and forth. Fingers and feet would involuntarily move either in synchronized patterns or alternating right, left, right, left. . . .

And when they'd open their eyes, they'd tell me that they were seeing colors they had never seen before; smelling fragrances, often floral, that they had never before smelled; seeing and hearing "people" who weren't in the room for anyone else to see or hear.

And then they started reporting healings. Real healings. They were getting up out of wheelchairs, some of them. They were regaining the use of arms, legs, vision, hearing. . . . Patients were bringing me in laboratory results showing that their cancer growths had vanished. And children with cerebral palsy and epilepsy were able to walk, run, and speak normally; no longer had seizures; no longer required medication. My patients and their doctors would call and ask, "What did you do?"

"Nothing," was my reply. "And don't tell anyone!"

It was like the government trying to tell people to "just say no" to drugs. The more I said it, the more people talked.

Soon people started asking me to teach this work. "Teach it?!" I responded. "How do you teach something like this?" *I stand there waving my hands in the air looking like an idiot,* I thought. I told them to "go outside, wave your hands in the air, and let me know what your neighbors have to say about it!"

Yet more and more of my patients would call me after their sessions to report that when they drove up to their homes, their automatic garage doors opened before they hit the little clicker buttons in their cars to open them. Or when they entered their homes, their TVs or sound systems turned themselves on and off and on and off. They felt sensations in their hands and held them near someone in their family who was having a problem, and *that person* had a healing!

And suddenly we began to recognize what science and researchers would later confirm: that once you interact with this new, broader, more comprehensive spectrum of healing frequencies, something changes within you that allows you to not only access your own healing, but to facilitate healing for others. Science today calls this *Reconnective Healing,* and this was the basis for my first book, *The Reconnection: Heal Others, Heal Yourself.*

So, back in the room with Fred, the breathy sounds continued as I watched, fascinated . . . perhaps *too* fascinated, as it suddenly dawned on me that I was spending far too long in the room with him while my other patients were waiting for me. I touched Fred lightly on his sternum with my index and middle fingers and softly said, "Fred, I think we're finished now."

Fred opened his eyes. He looked at me. I looked at him. He didn't say anything. So I didn't say anything. I mean, what was there really to say?

I can't tell you that I didn't think about it—*a lot*—for the rest of that week until his next visit. I was sure it was going to happen again. I scheduled all of my patients before Fred so I'd have some extra time in case it did.

And it did. I adjusted him, and told him to close his eyes and relax and allow the adjustment to settle. As he was lying there, I held my hands in the air near his head, and the scene from his previous visit was repeated. His head jerked back, eyes rolled back in his head, lips parted, tongue moved, and air audibly escaped from his mouth. But this time the air condensed itself into a voice. And the voice said: *"We are here to tell you to continue doing what you are doing. What you are doing is bringing light and information onto the planet."*

Fred looked at me and confessed that he had had that voice coming through him since he was approximately 11 years old; that only two people in his life knew about it; that he'd felt it starting up during his previous visit, but he thought that I didn't notice anything. I told him to relax and let it flow.

I thought that this was something unique to Fred. A "Fred thing." Little could I have anticipated what was to come next.

Two days later, three other patients lost consciousness and spoke the same two phrases that Fred had spoken: *"We are here to tell you to continue doing what you are doing. What you are doing is bringing light and information onto the planet."* However, a third and a fourth phrase were added. Two patients said: *"What you are doing is reconnecting strands."* One of them said: *"What you are doing is reconnecting strings."*

Fred came back in later for another visit and told me that while he was at home, he had been doing automatic writing. (Apparently another "Fred thing.") He said that it was his usual automatic writing, except for the last two sentences, which read: *Do not underestimate the power of Dr. Eric Scott Pearl. What he is doing is reconnecting strings.*

I asked him if he was sure it said "strings." I knew that *strands* meant DNA. *Strings* had to have been a mistake, I thought. Or perhaps some entity, some intelligence from the universe, was trying to communicate with me, and was somewhat encumbered by having to find words in the English language to convey a concept that was somewhere in between *strings* and *strands.* But Fred insisted that what he had written was *strings.*

By the way, did I tell you that none of these patients knew one another? Well, then let me tell you now: *None of these patients knew one another.* Nor did they know any of the five people it happened to in my office the following week. All in all, over the next three months, more than 50 different patients lost consciousness and spoke up to six of the same verbatim phrases.

What I soon recognized was that sometimes you're given the opportunity to walk through doors when you're not sure where they lead. Most often this is the case, and it is what happened with me.

From the beginning, I was spoon-fed fear disguised as love from "healers" watching from the outside. People would ask, "What's the source of these healings? Is it a good source?"

"Of course it is," I'd reply. "It's God. It's love. It's the universe."

"How do you know?" they would ask.

"I just know," I told them.

"But how do you know?" they would ask again, until *I* began to wonder how I knew. I mean I *knew.* I just didn't know *how* I knew. So, thinking that those who were posing these questions must know something that I didn't, I asked them how I should go about determining the source.

"Ask it," was their response.

Ask it? Ask it?! What kind of answer was that?! If you ask a good source if it's a good source, it tells you the truth and says it's a good source. If you ask a bad source if it's a good source, it lies and tells you it's a good source.

I mean, here were these healers who had the audacity to infuse fear where fear didn't belong, and didn't even have the integrity to give me proper guidance to get to the answer. *Ask it?!*

So I thought and I thought and I thought. And finally I came up with two worst-case scenarios:

(a) I die. I show up at the Pearly Gates or wherever we go, and St. Peter or whoever is supposed to be there is there and looks up my name in the Book of Life.

> *Eric Pearl . . . Eric Pearl . . . Eric Pearl . . . here it is. . . . Hmm . . . you led a lot of people down a very foolish path. You have to go back and live your life over again 600 times. . . .*

Well, let me tell you. That's not a very exciting possibility. But here comes the *worst* worst-case scenario:

(b) I die. I show up at the Pearly Gates or wherever, and St. Peter or whoever is there and looks up my name in the Book of Life.

> *Eric Pearl . . . Eric Pearl . . . Eric Pearl . . . here it is. . . . Hmm . . . we gave you an opportunity to bring about a change of consciousness that would have ripple effects throughout the universe in perpetuity. . . . And you didn't do it. . . . Because you were afraid. . . .*

You see, *that* was the choice I couldn't live with.

> *The light comes not from without, but from within. . . .*
> *Your life is providing that light.*
>
> — S O L O M O N

Through the teachings from Solomon—the entity whospeaks through the physical being of Fred—and my own evolution, I've come to understand what I call the *One-Cause Theory.* The One-Cause Theory posits that the degree to which we fall away from perfect health is the degree to which we've temporarily forgotten that we *are* the light. And all we need do is remember that we *are* that light, to remind ourselves in a way that allows us to return to our natural state of light vibration. And as we vibrate in our optimal state of light, anything denser than that light pretty much has nothing left to hold on to; therefore, it falls away, *if it is appropriate at that point on our life path for it to do so.*

I learned that being a healer—that is, facilitating healings for others—is a pretty pure experience. I learned to simply step into the equation with the other person and the universe, transcend technique entirely, and allow myself to *feel. Feel.* That is, to *listen* . . . with a different sense. To feel, observe, play, notice. Without judgment. And that's a huge part of the key. I learned that as we transcend technique, we transcend direction, we transcend specific pinpoint desired outcome, and we transcend judgment. I learned how to step out of my *results* orientation and instead step into a *process* orientation. And as I allowed myself to do so, I became more aware of the field, as well as my sensations. Varying sensations: hot, cold, wet, dry, pushing, pulling, bubbling, sparkling.

The funny thing about all of this is the simplicity of what underlies it. You see, as I distilled all of these sensations down, they became essentially one: joy, happiness . . . *bliss.* As I experienced that bliss, I stepped into the *field* and became one with it. And I discovered that we are not in the field alone. We are in the field with everyone . . . specifically, with that person who has our *attention,* because—let's face it—we go where our attention is, where our awareness is. Somehow in this interaction, consciously or otherwise, a little "voice"—figuratively speaking—inside that person says, *Hey, I remember this. This is me vibrating healthy. This is me vibrating as light. . . . I think I'll do it again.*

And in that remembrance, I watched as people began to vibrate at their optimal light level once more, and they began to vibrate healthy. I observed that anything denser than that light, which includes pretty much most health challenges, if appropriate for that person at that point in time on his/her life path, simply falls away. Immediately it became more than clear that healing is just that simple. And anything—*anything*—more complicated than that is designed to sell us something.

As I allowed myself to *listen*—to stop *doing* and instead to *become,* to become the observer and the observed—this is where and when the universe often chose to display its true wonder and its beauty. This is the gift. It is here that we see things that are new, that are different, that are real. Very, *very* real. We experience, then, each session with a sense of newness and discovery, because with each person, it *is* new.

Your job is to open doors.
Their job is to decide whether they
have the courage to walk through them.

— SOLOMON

You see, I don't like the word *healing.* It's far too limited in its common interpretation. *Healing* implies that there's something you have to get "better" from. I observed that healing is more than just getting up out of wheelchairs, regaining hearing or speech, cancer tumors vanishing, or cerebral-palsied children walking and talking normally. Although these are all more than wonderful and more than exciting when we witness them while doing this work, healing in its truest sense is much more than that. These "healings" are signs of something much larger. They're signs of our more comprehensive access to, and interaction with, the universe. They're signs of our evolution. A *Human Upgrade,* if you will.

Our existence is about our *continued* evolution. I've learned that life is about our ability to adapt and evolve. It's a continual process. Occasionally the process occurs so slowly, so subtly, that we don't notice it. Other times it takes leaps into obvious apparentness, and it's anything *but* subtle. . . .

As I allowed myself to simply witness and to "be," I observed that this is healing of a very different nature than we have been taught to perceive, understand, or even believe or accept. This healing is about an evolutionary process brought into existence through *co-creation* at the highest vibrational interaction with the universe, at the highest vibrational interaction with the field.

If a man would allot half an hour every night for
self-conversation, and recapitulate with himself whatever
he has done, right or wrong, in the course of the day, he
would be both the better and the wiser for it.

— PHILIP DORMER STANHOPE,
4TH EARL OF CHESTERFIELD (1694–1773)

My life has changed because of this work. I would like to be able to tell you precisely how it has changed, how *I* have changed—yet I don't really *know* how. Because I've been living with "me" day after day, I see more of my searching to be better than I see my actual achievements. I see myself when I handle a situation well, and it makes me feel good inside. I see myself when I don't handle a situation as well as I could have, and I feel hurt and disappointed in myself. And yet I persevere, determined to do better next time.

Do I see the majority of the messengers—that is, speakers and presenters—as *being* their message offstage? To varying degrees. That allows me to see that I am human, that we are all human. I don't have a different offstage and onstage persona, so you get me as I am: the good, the bad, and the ugly. But you get the truth. Am I as patient and understanding as I'd like to be? No. Am I more patient and understanding than I was? Absolutely. Would I like to *be* my message? Definitely. Am I? Well, I'm getting there. And possibly when I become my message, there will be little reason for me to be "in the body." But I have a long way to go, so I don't plan on departing this life very soon! I guess the biggest change for me is my willingness to observe myself—my actions, my inactions, my successes, my short-comings—with less judgment and the desire to improve. Maybe this is me reconnecting with the truth and purity of who I am as a being, as a soul.

We make our choices either out of fear or out of love. Fear, including lack, limitation, the illusion of separation and darkness . . . or love, including unity, abundance, prosperity, oneness, and light. I choose to make my choices out of love. Now, this is not always as easy as it sounds. And at times I wondered if I were doing the right thing. At times I wondered whether I was living in a dream and would wake up. Other times I simply wondered whether I was losing my mind or had lost it completely. Maybe I was in a hospital bed somewhere in a coma, and all of this was simply my imagination.

Yet, when I found myself in doubt, I reminded myself that I wasn't the one who spoke those original six phrases. It was over 50 different people. And none of them except Fred had ever had a voice come through them before. I knew that the answers were there. In the phrases. They became my mantras to see me through the times when I doubted myself or the situation. I would keep them posted somewhere easy for me to see so that when I began to doubt, I could find just the right phrase to help me through those periods. I give them to you here so that you can have a copy of them for your own use.

1. *We are here to tell you to continue doing what you are doing.*

2. *What you are doing is bringing light and information onto the planet.*

3. *What you are doing is reconnecting strings.*

4. *What you are doing is reconnecting strands.*

5. *You must see/know that you are a master.*

6. *We've come because of your reputation.*

In a sense, I used these as mantras. They worked for me. And I hope that they work for you!

But please keep in mind that although the six phrases are very key to understanding this work, they are not the main focus of this book. You are more than welcome to read about them and their meaning in *The Reconnection*. The significance of this occurrence for the purpose of this Prologue is that the voices, the phrases, *stopped* happening. Just about. Sort of. In a way. And yet the information continued to come through Fred in a far more expanded manner.

I would go to Fred periodically and ask if I could speak to that voice that came through him. Fred didn't always like to bring the voice through, but with sufficient encouragement, he would sometimes acquiesce. And I had the forethought to record those sessions.

During the first and second sessions, including the "I Want You to Wonder" sequence that this book opens with, we used three tape recorders . . . and all three continually broke down. So I finally invested in a quality recording system to get every word. Then I had the tapes transcribed so that they could be read. I kept them safely stored, starting in 1994, as I wasn't sure how to properly share the material, or if I should do so at all.

Over the years and a few moves, Fred and I lost touch. And in 2008 or so, after some extensive research, I located him. A couple of years later we decided to collaborate to bring this material to the public.

As you go through this book, you will find many more phrases and insights to help carry you along. Not only as a Reconnective Healer, but as a reconnected person, for this book is about reconnecting *your* life. It is designed to transform not only those who want to become healers, real healers . . . but to transform each of us who is looking to reconnect and bring about world harmony in this time.

PROLOGUE

Fred's Story

A Note from Eric Pearl: You may already be familiar with me, Reconnective Healing, and The Reconnection, but you may not yet be familiar with my co-author, Frederick Ponzlov, and the role he played in bringing through certain information and insights that have the capacity to transport us to deeper and more comprehensive levels as healers and as people. While I touched upon this briefly in my own Prologue, I felt it only appropriate to bring you Fred's story as well, in his own words. . . .

I seldom remember beginnings. But at some point it began . . . in rural Wisconsin on a farm. The clearest memory was when I was ten and I was falling asleep, or thought I was asleep, and heard my closet door open. I sat up in my bed and suddenly heard a whirring sound that increased in volume and pitch, and just when I thought it couldn't get any louder or any higher-pitched, I felt something move into my body.

I, of course, was terrified, but couldn't scream because I didn't have control of my vocal apparatus. I felt my mind racing through my body, running down into my feet and running out into my hands, trying to find some physical sensation that I still had control of. As it turned out, nothing was responding. I was literally paralyzed with fear. My breathing became shallower, and before long it seemed as if I were just panting.

Then suddenly it felt as if my body was covered by a long, white wet sheet. Slowly, it started to be lifted from my feet first. But it was agonizingly slow. As soon as it got past my toes, I could feel sensation in my feet, and I wiggled my toes madly. Then as every part of my body was slowly being reclaimed, I could feel the bodily sensations that were again mine. And when the sheet lifted past my throat, I screamed.

The year was 1962, and there was no frame of reference for any of this. But it was as real for me as the proverbial heart attack.

Several weeks later, on a warm August day, I awoke to the sounds of a man screaming in the distance. It felt as if it came from the yard, so I jumped out of bed as the screaming continued and raced out to the lawn along the side of our house. The screaming continued. I was standing in my underwear but couldn't discern a clear direction from which the shrieking emanated. Our closest neighbors were each a half mile away, and I thought that perhaps some accident had occurred on one of their farms.

But then . . . nothing. It stopped. The screaming. And I stood dazed in wonder, my feet damp from the early-morning dew.

Several days later I found out that a former hired hand from our farm had on that very morning gone to start up his new employer's tractor and wasn't aware that it was still in gear. The tractor jerked as it started and lunged forward but was blocked by the retaining wall, and the hired hand was caught underneath the spinning rear tire. They said his screams were deafening. The tire worked its way through his body, and then the friction of the wheel on the cement started the shed on fire and he was prematurely cremated.

The only problem was that this happened *15 miles* away.

When the story eventually reached my ears, I knew that something was different—with me. But there was no one I could confide this to, and I was unsure how to even convey what I didn't understand.

I still don't understand.

Around the age of 13, I remember reading about, or hearing about, automatic writing. Again clueless, I would close my eyes and put a pen in my hand as I hoped that something would come through. And I could feel my hand moving across the page. Yet when I opened my eyes, it all was just a scrawl, with no discernible words that I could grasp at the time. I saved the very first card I wrote, and returning to it years later, there, clearly in the middle of the scrawl, was the word *Energy.*

Sometimes you can't see something until you need to see it.

I went away to college, to the University of Wisconsin–Milwaukee; majored in theater; and had several of what could be called *psychic phenomena* occur, chalking them all up to coincidence. I then moved to New York City to pursue a career as an actor, and one summer got a job at the Colorado Shakespeare Festival, in Boulder.

Once there, I realized that not only were we on the campus of the University of Colorado, but right next door was the Naropa Institute (a Buddhist-inspired university combining contemplative studies with traditional Western disciplines), and this had become the summer of Transcendental Meditation (TM). A good friend from New York coincidentally happened to be at Naropa for a summer session, and told me all about TM. I wanted to enroll but, being an actor, didn't have the coinage to purchase for myself my own mantra. So I co-opted "Om" because I'd heard that was a mantra. As always, I had no idea what I was doing but sat cross-legged every morning, "Oming" away, waiting for something to happen or my mind to settle or whatever was supposed to occur.

Then, one morning after I had given up any hope for any tangible result, something did happen. I had just been breezily pondering a question in my unquieted mind, and an answer came. *But . . .* it wasn't "my" answer. It was something else. *Someone* else. Someone talking in a way that wasn't remotely the way I spoke. I tentatively responded to the voice, and another answer came, then another question, then another answer.

I stopped for a moment and clearly thought, *How great is this? Congratulations, you have just become a schizophrenic!* I blamed Colorado: the elevation, the pressure from the shows, and perhaps not feeling at ease in my surroundings.

And then there was the problem with writing longhand in those pre-computer days. I never had any problem prior to that, but suddenly I was challenged to form letters in a handwriting that was mine. Sometimes it would go off and spell other words. This started becoming annoying.

I survived Colorado and returned to New York. Shortly afterward, I got caught in the turbulent wake of two murders, having arrived on the scene after each had occurred. I went to two separate psychics, when I still believed in psychic inevitability, to make sense of what was happening. Both told me with great urgency to leave New York—it was *not* the city for me to be in at the moment.

I had never thought of going to Los Angeles, where my former roommate had moved just eight months earlier. She encouraged me to come out and stay with her to pursue the "acting thing" on the West Coast. I had never, ever contemplated living on the "left coast" and still possessed that right-coast snobbery about living in a state with the culturally unwashed. But after the events that had recently occurred, I thought maybe it was time to take the psychics' advice and get out of Dodge. So I packed my Rambler, which I'd recently inherited from my wonderful aunt, and eventually made it to Route 10 and followed it to its logical conclusion.

Once in L.A., I immediately set about looking for a place to live, and I had no idea what area was preferable, not knowing the layout of the city. A week later I settled into an apartment with a Murphy bed that was only a block from Grauman's Chinese Theatre. I thought it couldn't get much more Hollywood than this.

I had moved all my unpacked boxes into one corner and was about to start going through them when, while I sat on the fold-out bed, the room started to move and shake. I thought it was stress from the trip westward. In actuality, it was my first earthquake. It passed almost as quickly as it started.

After catching my breath, I decided to unpack a box of books, and the book on the very top was *The Nature of Personal Reality*, by Jane Roberts. I had started reading it in New York and had put a bookmark in it to continue once I was firmly, or now somewhat firmly, rooted in La-La land. I casually opened to the bookmarked page where I had left off and started reading. The chapter was about why people move to areas where earthquakes occur.

After taking it in and unpacking some more boxes, I decided I would take a nap. I lay my head down, and 15 minutes later I woke up with a start. There, at the base of the bed, was an old woman sitting with a shawl over her head and around her shoulders. My first reaction was: how did this homeless woman, one of the many who populated the streets of Hollywood in those days, get into my room with my door locked? She turned and smiled directly at me, and then she literally faded away. Disappeared as I was looking at her.

Welcome to Hollywood.

In Jane Roberts's book, she channeled a spirit named Seth. I was dubious about a lot of it—but, like anything, there were little insights here and there that I thought I could use. At one point Seth suggested that if you wanted to have a memory of a former life, the thing to do was to make a conscious suggestion before going to sleep of having a dream about a pleasant former life, which you would then be able to remember in the morning.

Well, the first couple of nights . . . *nada.* Nothing happened. Then on the third night, I had this amazingly vivid dream of being at a party at Harold Lloyd's in the late '20s. First of all, I barely knew who Harold Lloyd was. All I knew was that he was a silent-film star and was the figure dangling from the hands on the clock in that iconic picture. But beyond that, not much.

Anyway, in the dream I am at this party, and it's a very big mansion. I look at Harold Lloyd, who doesn't seem to be having a particularly happy time, and I turn to the person I came with, a photographer, and I say, "Why is Harold Lloyd so unhappy?"

She looks at me and then says, "He has a very dark personality."

And then I woke up.

I thought, *Who in the world dreams about Harold Lloyd and his dark personality?* That day I told a number of friends, who were as bemused as I was, and we all laughed it off.

Then several days later, early in the morning, I made my way to where my Rambler last rested, and I found only an empty space. The car was gone. Of course I panicked and thought that someone had stolen it, and the next thought replacing that one was: *Who would steal a Rambler?*

Nonetheless, I called the police to report this grievous act, and was informed that the car had not been stolen but towed, due to the Wisconsin license plates that had expired. I, of course, was none too happy about this turn of events and had to bike my way to Beverly Hills to pay the ticket to free my Rambler from the clutches of a very proactive police department.

I had never been to the Beverly Hills City Hall. As I walked down the long corridor, on either side were pictures of the huge estates that were ubiquitous in the '20s in Beverly Hills. I gazed at one picture and it stopped me cold.

I thought, *I know this estate, I do; I know this estate.* I looked down at the bottom of the picture to see whose it was. There, in a clear Roman font, were the words: THE ESTATE OF HAROLD LLOYD.

I gasped just slightly, then gasped even louder as I looked down the hall at the next picture. There, in a very formally posed photograph, was Harold Lloyd at a party, along with every single one of the people who were in my dream, wearing the exact same clothes that I remembered them wearing. I was totally mystified.

I stared at the picture a very long time and finally moved forward, remembering the reason why I was in the hallway in the first place. But glancing back at the picture, I wondered if maybe the reason the Rambler had been towed was for me to see this. Of course, I deferred to my rational mind and reasoned that perhaps this picture was printed in a book somewhere, and my subconscious mind had picked it up and spun a dream around it.

Yes, that makes sense to me, I thought as I moved up to the window to pay the fine, where my wallet got considerably lightened.

✖

Several days later, a friend called me up and told me I had to go see this psychic who lived in Simi Valley. She told me how remarkable he was and that without fail he guessed everyone's birthday.

Well, I wasn't sure what the appeal was in having someone guess another person's birthday, but I was intrigued. I had no idea where Simi Valley was. I got on the road and drove for what seemed endless miles.

It always takes longer on the journey to the unknown.

I pulled up to a weathered little house in need of painting, with the address barely visible above the bougainvillea. I knocked on the door and there was no answer. I was a little upset, as the journey out to this hinterland was not without getting lost two or three times in these pre-MapQuest years, and way before the letters *GPS* had any meaning. To anyone.

I walked around to the back of the house, and there, sitting at an old Formica kitchen table with his back to me, was a still older man wearing bib overalls. He reminded me of a Santa Claus who'd come upon hard times. I asked him if he knew the guy whose name was on a piece of paper I was holding in my hand.

He told me that the name was his, and asked me to sit down next to him. A few roaming chickens crossed my path before I could get to the chair he pulled out for me.

Now at this point I was really dubious about this guy because he didn't fit the profile I had in my mind for someone who was in touch with the other side, should there *be* an "other side."

He looked at me a long time, and then put his head down to think.

Now, my birthday happens to be April 2nd. My mother was taken to the hospital Sunday, the 1st of April, because she had gone into a semblance of labor. But they couldn't locate the doctor, and since I was going to be a cesarean, they couldn't go forward with the birth. So they waited until Monday, the 2nd, when said doctor could be located, and I was born at 8:01 that morning.

So now I was sitting across from this weathered old man, wondering what the point of all of this was.

He slowly raised his head. "This has never happened to me before," he said, "but I am getting two dates. I'm getting April 1st, but you were born April 2nd—is that correct?"

I blanched, and stuttered out a mystified "Yes."

He then looked me straight in the eye, and the very next thing he uttered was, "You have a strange connection to Harold Lloyd. Has anyone ever told you that?"

I was in absolute shock. I hardly heard a word of what he said after that, wondering how in the hell, of all the people who are out there, living and dead, he could come up with the name Harold Lloyd.

I made my way back to Hollywood and seeming sanity. I couldn't wrap my head around how this man knew what he knew.

Now, all during this time, the voice that I heard in Colorado would sometimes surface, and I would either ignore it or pretend that I didn't hear what I was hearing. Then late in 1992, I visited a friend who was going through quite an emotionally challenging time. As I talked to her, I felt as if someone or something was trying to take over the conversation from within me, and this presence got stronger and I began to feel very spacey and drowsy.

I finally said to her that I felt "someone or something" wanted to communicate something to her, and I felt as if I were losing my consciousness. Would she mind my stepping back for a moment?

As the feeling grew stronger, my friend's golden retriever starting whining, then barking, getting very anxious. I finally seemed to pass out, but was aware that someone was using my vocal mechanism, and I could feel my hands and arms gesturing. I didn't understand what was being said, and that feeling continued for some time. I finally felt the presence leave, and I returned to consciousness, albeit drowsily.

I looked at my friend, whose jaw had dropped to somewhere near the middle of her chest. I felt as if I had awakened from a deep sleep. I asked her what had happened, and she said little on the subject but explained that it all was very personal. She seemed very moved and mystified. I did not pressure her any further.

I left feeling extremely uncomfortable and, I have to admit, a little scared. I wasn't sure how this phenomenon would be received by other people should it happen again, and I determined at that time that I would keep all of this to myself. (Years later my friend told me that the spirit had discussed a child she had given up when she was very young.)

Sometime later I got a job coordinating the "OUTAuction" fundraiser in Los Angeles. It was an immense undertaking, and after it was over, for some reason I ended up with three sessions with a chiropractor by the name of Eric Pearl. I had never been to a chiropractor prior to that and wasn't even sure exactly what a chiropractor did, but it was California, and I thought it was part of the experience that was Los Angeles.

I entered the office on Melrose Place and sat in the comfortable, cozy lobby. I was ushered into a small room, where I waited with great trepidation. Then Dr. Pearl entered, and my first thought was that this man didn't look anything like a doctor. But I lay down on his table, and before I knew it, this drowsy sensation started coming over me and I fought to stay awake. I thought I couldn't afford to fall asleep on my first visit. It would be poor form.

All through the adjustment, I continued my battle against falling asleep and wondered how I would get through the next two visits. And sure enough, on the next visit the very same thing started happening, only the battle to stay awake was harder fought. I didn't know how to reference this and wasn't sure if I should even mention these sensations to the good doctor.

Before the next session I did alert Dr. Pearl to this phenomenon and asked him if it was symptomatic of the chiropractic process. He looked at me, slightly bemused, but fascinated. He suggested I not fight the feeling but instead surrender to it.

I did. And this book is what has resulted from my continuing sessions with him.

Do I understand what happens? No, I don't. I only know that I lose a consciousness of a sort, and when I awake, I sometimes remember a word, a bit of a phrase here and there, but nothing more than that.

I have shared Solomon, a name we bestowed upon the voice, to many other people who have happened into my environment who are lost or are needing guidance. But in Eric's case, Solomon had a clear mission for him, and his guidance has led to the sessions that appear in this book, and ultimately, the Reconnective Healing that Dr. Pearl has pioneered. I believe Solomon's message to be universal, but *you* will be the final judge on that. . . .

INTRODUCTION

Before you continue on to the actual material that Fred and I have committed to these pages for you, allow me to share some discoveries I made on my journey through this book that might give you some ideas as to how to utilize it most effectively.

Solomon, a name we ascribed to the consciousness and intelligence that imparted this information to us, is actually the sum total of two different entities. We dubbed the intelligence that first spoke through Fred, and over 50 of my other patients, *Aaron.* Relatively soon into the sessions, the voice, the intelligence, we characterize as Solomon appeared. We've elected, for ease of communication, to refer to the information collectively as the "Solomon" information; that is, the voice of the information, whether through Aaron or Solomon, is known as Solomon. Most of the material in this book originated with Aaron and Solomon, and they chose here to speak through Fred. In essence, you can think of Fred as the telephone and Aaron and Solomon as the callers. We—you and I—can be considered the recipients of the phone call!

The chapters of Solomon speaking are verbatim wherever we could make that possible. Each chapter for the most part was a separate session, and the sessions appear in the order they were given. In some cases we have combined parts of sessions where similar topics were addressed in separate readings.

You may notice that Solomon speaks in a rhythm, grammar, and syntax that might seem a little foreign at first. Here, punctuation is but mere suggestion (although I wouldn't advise explaining that to your fourth-grade English teacher!). Solomon will sometimes speak in the first-person singular ("I") and other times in the first-person plural ("we"). Oftentimes he will say things with great emphasis, and we have made an attempt to italicize these words to give you a more specific sense of his deliberate meaning.

As well, Solomon will repeat points throughout the book. Realize that this material spans many years and represents many sessions held during that time. Points needed to be made, and made again. Although we have kept this to a minimum, where we feel that Solomon selected certain points to be reiterated, we have left some of this repetition in the material. My belief is that by keeping it as close to the original as possible, we can better share with you the intensity and intention of the experience and the message.

The fact is, sometimes *I* just needed to hear it again. You might say that I wasn't necessarily the easiest student. I had to process the information, to experience it and to challenge myself—at times when a challenge wasn't what I was consciously looking for—in order to come to a truer understanding of it. In reality, this was guidance given to me in the process of becoming a healer. Yet it is so much more than that. It has shown itself to me to be insights that resonate in every aspect of my life.

This material is written on many, many levels. That is part of what makes reading it so very fascinating: The layers of meaning. The layers of *potential* meaning. The doors that open for us to walk through. Even though I was present at each of the sessions, I find that as I read and reread the material, I gain more and more depth of insight. For many, this material is not easily absorbed in one reading. And if you're like me, you will choose to revisit it again and again. At times I like to read the book straight through to appreciate the sequential development. At other times I like to simply open it to a page and see where my instinct leads me on that day. Often the synchronicity between what comes up in the book and what comes up in my life that day is awe-inspiring, presenting me with just the answers I didn't even know I was looking for.

From my own experience, I have found it to be a good idea to journal and note my thoughts and insights as I read and reread the Solomon material. After each chapter, I encourage you to jot down your notes, questions, or impressions in a journal or notebook. For me, this gives me time and focus to absorb what I have experienced in the reading. I also find it fascinating to look back on what I wrote 12 years ago—or even 12 *months* ago—and see how my perspectives and insights have evolved. For this reason I wrote the dates by each of my journaling entries. In writing and putting this together, I found it best for me not to rush through the book, but to take it in in bite-size chunks, to give myself space between the chapters to "breathe in" what has been said and reflect upon how this applies to many of my particular life experiences. The journaling helped me do that.

At times I've noticed that some of the material appears to contradict itself. As I've read deeper . . . looked deeper . . . searched deeper, I've found that I suddenly see how seeming opposites become one, unified. And then I wonder how I missed it the first time or three! I find this material so timeless and ever expansive that it is my plan to read this book many more times throughout my life.

What also became clear to Fred and me—and to the many who graciously gave their time and input in reading through this material so that we could find the very best way to present it to you—was the added side benefit of a feeling of well-being and healing just by absorbing the information. This will vary, of course, with each individual, but it is something that we believe you may tangibly experience as well.

These sessions were part of *my* growth as Reconnective Healing emerged. And yet I have found them so far to be vital to everyone—relevant not only to anyone learning healing or undertaking a role in the healing world, but to anyone seeking to understand life in general. So even though at times it might appear as if the material is addressing me specifically or only healers, know that it is universal in its application. This takes you along on my ups and my downs; it spotlights my areas of growth, evolution, and success, as well as areas where there is room, often *much* room, for further growth, evolution, and success. At times this may appear to be laudatory of me—of *us*—and at times critical. I believe the intent of the communication to be neither. This is intended to shine a light on our potential, our newly expanded potential for a newly expanded time. And it is to remind us that as we travel our life path, with its ups and its seeming downs, we are each a blessing. And we are *definitely* not alone.

As you read *Solomon Speaks on Reconnecting Your Life* today, allow yourself to *hear it speaking to you.* Because it *is.* It is speaking *directly* to you. This book is not fortune-telling, nor does it predict the future. These are *life* insights that allow each and every one of us to access and facilitate a greater level of healing for ourselves and for others, because it shows us how to access greater and deeper levels of ourselves and of others. In other words, to reconnect, to *heal others*, to *heal yourself.*

As Solomon tells us, "We are all one." So, as I take you along on my journey, I hope that you will find parts of *your* journey here as well. Enjoy the scenery. This is a work of love. Walk . . . walk through the doors.

— Eric Pearl

I want you to wonder. . . .

I want you to realize another plane . . .

part of a much greater plane. . . .

You have always been part of the cycle. . . .

You are here to facilitate your perception. . . .

You are coming into a plateau of existence. . . .

We have much to understand in this space.

1

WHO IS SOLOMON?

A Note from Eric and Fred: What you read on the preceding page was an early message that was given to us through Solomon. We were curious as to who exactly Solomon was, and in our sessions we asked him specifically for an identity. We thought it best if we allowed him to just introduce himself to you. . . .

We have *all* met before, and here we are. No accident, is it? You have to see that our lives are united in a very deep and complex manner. It's an interwoven tapestry of existence. And it's beautiful. We will work together. We will be brave in the doing of it.

We are fond of names. It is of little consequence to me by which you call me forward. The name Solomon was attached to me arbitrarily through Fred and Eric's device. If Solomon is convenient, that is perfectly acceptable. Aaron likes his name very much. It's very likable.

I'm very much a part of that spiritual realm that can be labeled *Aaron,* and Aaron is very involved in what might be labeled, as you refer to me, *Solomon.* I am not an entity the way you perceive. I use this body to communicate a wealth of knowledge that comes through the experience of many, many energies. I am a product of that agreement of energy. This is just the manifestation, not what it is. It is like the wind blowing through the trees. The wind isn't the sound of the trees rustling, but that sound is the manifestation of it. It talks in a language that you can understand. But in actuality, what really is happening with all of this—in this space now—is the energy transfer. That's what is qualitative. The words are recognizable, but there is another energy transfer that is going on that is deeper, that is more profound. We are entities that have amassed a great confluence of energy that is helping those who must find their way in this point in time, where things are going to change rapidly. They are here, and we are here to unveil the change and be able to help them deal with it as it reveals itself.

In essence, we are all of a great entity of the same energy, so I don't want to lead you wrong in thinking that we are very distinct personalities. On one level we are; but on another, *greater* picture, we are of *one* force. We bloom in different ways.

I'm trying to find a way to help you visualize. We are of a common blood. Our force has been the force of eternity. Our lives manifest this eternity in different realms. We are at one with our lives, and we are at one with eternity.

I come from an energy source that has been in time. It has been in the inception of life itself. It is a plane of existence that has never been touched until recently. It has come because the alarm has sounded.

It comes in a way that is fundamental to our greater understanding of the forces that operate within the universe. Our entity, as it were, is a family of energies that converge. There are many members of this family; Fred and Eric happen to each be one, as do you. We have missions, as it were, in various planes. Our mission here is of a very urgent nature: the need for people to understand their roles in the universe. There is a great time ahead. But great struggle to it as well.

We have been here for you before. We have always been here. We will be a part of That Which Is as we carry you in our hearts. We feel your energy.

I am only an intermediary to greater energy. I am part of that energy, and I am handing it to you. It is there to help. I am as much a conduit as you are. We are a chain leading to the center, That Which Is.

I am representative of another facet of that energy. We are *many* individuals in one force field. We are expressing various facets of a greater truth as it is unveiled.

You might ask if I'm a personality, because I am personable in this interaction. If I were to be here and just allow you to experience it, there would be value, but you wouldn't recognize it.

So in other words, I speak through Fred—and through that, people somehow are validated, because I have no judgment issues with anyone. I am not about judging anyone. I'm only there to help them remember who they are and the greatness they are and that greatness that is in all human life-forms and the respect with which somebody should be treated. Once that is fully realized, then you do have paradise.

2

I WANT YOU TO WONDER

I want you to wonder. . . . I want you to realize another plane . . . part of a much greater plane. . . . You have always been part of the cycle. . . . You are here to facilitate your perception. . . . You are coming into a plateau of existence. . . . We have much to understand in this space.

You understand something that will carry you to another experience. This is just the beginning of a tantalizing journey.

I have been here with you before. I want you to understand that there is no danger in reaching out, yet you must characterize your facility in a way that is in rhythm with the universe; you can't just understand with your logic.

The music of your life is in your instinct.

Your life is as meaningful as your ability to reach out. It is this search that endows you.

Energy is That Which Is in your life; in all instances, it is pervasive. It is not to be threatened or beguiled.

You are a novitiate of this world. This is your apprentice time.

I wish you to understand. You live your life. . . . It is written in your experience; it has a foundation that is clearly, distinctly, your own path. You see, it cannot be preordained.

This is of your being, that these energies flow through you. I am not only a part, but a participant, in this exchange that's not outside you. It's inside you.

I want you to feel that this force is palpable. Feel it. Can you feel it? It's there for you to access. It is a channel to wisdom that is looking at you, to a greatness that exists in space. You hear it with your life. It is incumbent that you desire this force, for it's what is the greatness of all existence.

You have a heart that is ready to be opened.

It is a difficult responsibility to bear, you know. It is overwhelming in many ways, but it will accentuate the life force you already possess. Energy is the key to connect you to a greater hope.

You have a force of nature coming through you—and your hands— that responds to environmental stimuli. It is a two-way encounter. It comes in, it flows through, it goes out. And in that interchange, you will understand the existence you so long to desire.

Many can reach this, but eyes are blind, you know. It is only a few who dare to open their eyes, and often those who do are blinded by what they see.

The kind of knowledge you seek is written in your heart. It is not outside you.

In looking to access it, I wish you the utmost inner quest. However, it is *your* quest. It will become clearer as you move forward. It is in transition and in your life. *You will feel discrepancies intertwine in a way that you don't want them to. It is not always your clear desire.* There will be a recognition of a palpable force. It will feel clearer as time goes on. These are such difficult times, you know. And so many hearts remain detached. Your mission, in a way, is to connect a spiritual heart to a spiritual existence. It's not always an easy thing you undertake. But it is the quest of life, you see. You must allow yourself a different space. It is time to feel much more. Allow this life force to pervade you.

3

FLOW FORWARD

I feel that we have all been here before. A reunion of sorts, you know. We have reached out to one another in a different field, but here we are. I have understood your coming from a different space, from unending Source. I feel a kind of effervescence flow. It is a part of you. I have heard you before. You have the need to communicate much. I have an energy that has come from a different universe. It is not of importance in terms of physical manifestations.

We, in essence, have all united in the past; and it is from these consensual hearts that we must wage our mission into this life here. It is, in essence, a form in which we manifest this energy. It is this form that we take that allows the interchange between you and me. It isn't the manifestation, but the exchange of energy.

There is such suffering happening in the world, and our suffering leads us away if we allow it, but we too often negate our suffering and somehow become victim to it. Suffering can bring immense joy—if it is focused. The lessons we exchange are those that continue from lifetime unto lifetime.

I feel your need is to understand that which is real. It is not an easy comprehension to come by. It is an energy that has come from an eternity.

Creation is such that it comes from an unequal and unparallel force. It is not of this understanding. It is manifest at moments when we create out of love and beneficence. Malevolence is only a twisted rope. It only needs to be stretched out and straightened, really.

Energy is a pool from which we drink. Are we thirsty? The nature of thirst determines that which comes to you.

We sometimes feel there is a separateness between us. That is where we often err in our understanding. We are all here as one. We flower in different fields. We come from the same soil. I want you to understand, if it is your will to understand, that we have our own vibration . . . but we are of the same sound. We all have the music of life, if you will, in all our actions. We all run into disharmony when we feel our energy taken away. It is a sense of a realm of abandonment. It is the child who turns around and she is alone—left to what we think are our own devices. We lose our way. Always this hurts. It can be healed, however. The voice that rises up from within you is the voice that heals you.

It is essential to persevere, in spite of our palette that is limited in color. There are other colors. We will discover them, but we are limited in this plane, yes. And perhaps you may feel you have a limitation in your heart that must be dispersed. But it comes from within your heart. That is where your work needs to be. I wish I had access for you. That would be a propheted kind of answer. But it is the nature of this question that needs to be undertaken. It is an orientation toward experience. Without this, there is very little growth in what we find in this plane. It is very frustrating to see such incredible potential thwarted. We have the power to unite, yet we seek to divide. It is very unfortunate.

I understand your desire, and that desire warms me. I feel I want to embrace you all, but we have to embrace our lives individually and then unite. We have such power.

Flow forward. Flow forward. Like a wave, it cannot be stopped. It moves. I wish you well.

★ ◇ ★

4

OUR INSTINCT IS THE SUM TOTAL OF ALL THAT IS

I feel you here. There is much I want to say to you. We have been here before with you. We feel your need reaching out to us. We want you to feel this energy flow through you.

Interaction between species is crucial to understanding this life. We have become dissociated from one another, you know. That is why the ability to reach out is crucial to this existence. You must understand—we are here to help one another, and we'll continue to do this. That is why you are here. You are reaching out. You should be very proud of that. You are connected spiritually to a greater source that comes through you.

Your hearts are here to fill each other. Your life is that of great necessity to be discovered. We mustn't close our eyes anymore. There's too much suffering being experienced needlessly. Your lives are in a state of transition. You are in a flux of sorts.

For example, it is no accident that earthquakes appear. We look upon these events as being separate from ourselves, and they really aren't. They are really a manifestation of change happening in every single one of us. The result is an earthquake. And earthquakes in our lives. These quakes make us all reevaluate our lives in a deep way. They are catalysts for all of you. They bring light, although it may be frightening.

But change can be frightening. It is so much easier to experience sadness; *that* we are comfortable with. It is change. It is actually a physical manifestation of a deeper earthquake. A spiritual one.

There is energy that gets transmitted. It is cyclical in nature. It is transmitted in different ways and takes different forms. When water becomes ice, it becomes a new creation. But really it's still water.

So in our lives, we metamorphose in various forms. And each form can be looked upon as a creation. But in actuality it is an energy transfer. It has always been. So in our narrow perspective in this plane, we see a baby and we think of it as a new creation. It's very ancient, that baby.

Were you to ask me if there is a beginning, there isn't one. There is That Which Is—we feel it here; we create it there. But it is impossible on this plane to explain this very complicated, difficult question when the answer is really in our instinct.

Our instinct is the sum total of All That Is. We clear a path. That instinct . . . *that* is what guides us. Trusting the instinct and discovering it.

I want to emphasize the connections we all have. Reinforce them. Without them we have lost. There is a great movement now to become isolated. Virtual reality, virtual sex, information superhighway. These are all aimed at cutting us off from one another.

You will find that there is going to be a rebellion in this technology. But it's based on fear. Communicable disease, crime . . . soon we won't look out anymore. And we must—we have to be open.

There is a collective mission here. That mission, in essence, is reaching out in any way you can. It's so important. That contact, that interaction, is where information is exchanged, more than on a verbal plane. It is energy being exchanged.

If the quality of energy is of a high plane, it gets exchanged. And it blossoms in another individual. And it's not what's being said. It's the intent.

So by reaching out from a higher perspective, we are creating a higher energy among us all. And that higher energy comes from instinct—our instinct. And clearing the path to it cannot be underestimated, though there is a problem sometimes of "Are our ears listening to 'instinct,' or are they listening to 'negative voices'?" The quest for instinct will define it for you.

We are about accessing information, all of us. We access it. Process it. And exchange it. It goes out into the world like a pebble thrown into the water, creating ripples of effect. That is what you do by creating value.

We need to throw those pebbles. The world will change. That is why we are here. It is of prime importance. That is why you showed up. You didn't pick up this book by accident. You are the reason! You must discover that. I wouldn't be here otherwise.

5

THERE IS A UNIVERSAL TRUTH
TO EVERY MOMENT OF LIFE

We want you to know that we are here for you. We have come here to help you. Our lives are united. We have much to exchange in this short period of time. We have greatness involved in this process. We must unite in a way to bring about a clearing.

You have started this work, and it's crucial for you to help integrate all that you take in. *This energy pool is vast.* It comes through all of us. It is essential that we take care of this energy. That we nurture it.

There is a transition going on right now. It is important that it organically appear, that it contact the lives we touch. It is looking for fertile soil. The seeds will grow in that fertile soil. They have to be nurtured. Cared for. We mustn't cast our seeds in the wind. There is certain soil that is fertile. We must seek out that soil. It will come to us organically, and needn't be thought of especially. It will appear, but it is important that we recognize fertility and infertility.

You must continue in this work to turn the page. The pages will appear for themselves. You must be intent on turning the pages of this book, as it were. We mustn't stop or feel stuck in any given chapter or anticipate what's to come. It will reveal itself organically.

There's a certain impatience going on because there's such crisis everywhere. We must hurry, but there *is* a plan. It needs to be organically conveyed and revealed in life; otherwise it has no meaning.

There's a complacency that occurs through a resistance that people have when they come in touch with the energy. They'll desire it, but when they come in touch with the energy, they go into reaction, and they start to resist and then go into complacency.

Well, it's denial. On a large scale, that denial needs to be dissipated out of their lives. It is the process that they must undertake. You can be there like a father, but you can't *take* them there.

They will come to it if they need to come to it. And they will. Sometimes not especially at the time you want. The patience I speak of . . .

As well, it needs to come in its own rhythm. There is a song to be sung. That comes with practice. The melody reveals itself as we deal with it.

It's a process. So, like a baby, you feed it one spoonful at a time. And then you watch it grow.

There is an energy that comes organically from your own life force.

There is a universal truth to every moment of life. There are millions of versions of that universal truth that happens in every moment. It comes from unity with the energy in our lives. When you're not in the way, you clear the way for that universal truth. That's what touches people's lives.

There is much to come. It will happen organically. It will happen on its own. It is going to be wonderful. Everything is revealed in its own rhythm.

You're way ahead of the game. You have felt this in your life before. You're not here by accident. These paths we are on are all somewhat similar yet distinctly our own. Yet we keep asking the person on the other path, "What do you feel over there? . . . What's around the corner?"

I don't know.

That's understandable. But then the directional signs show up when we need them. What I need or what you need becomes scarcely different. We don't give answers. We only give ways to utilize answers. If that answer lies in your instinct, it's *your* answer. *Yours.* It must come from your *own* life, and it will. Make no mistake. And you won't miss the sign. So you just have to keep your eyes open, always open.

That's the problem with the people in denial. "I don't see any signs. There's no sign. I don't see any . . ." And we understand their suffering about it. You want to shake them. *They* need to wake up and take the blinders off. *They* need to reach up and take the blinders off. *You* can't pull them off.

All in its time. Everything in its time. It's coming faster. It's very gratifying. There is so much open now, because our world at this present state is so devoid of hope. It *needs* to come back. And *in this search* is the answer.

Removing the blinders, for many, will come very fast. It is going to happen. It will be a fad at first. In some circles, it is now. People feel they *should* be doing it by peer pressure, but they will experience reality for themselves. They will feel it for themselves, and then they won't be looking to the next person to see if what they are doing is correct. Their lives will reveal it.

Let's keep our focus on the process. When you focus on the "when," you're putting the cart before the horse; you're thinking of the result and not the process.

Process *gets* result. Not the other way around. The purpose of the process is the process, not the result. If we gave you result, you might interpret it and corrupt the result. The result is the gift of the process. *Process.* That's where we become strong. The path you are on is taking you somewhere special, and it will open your heart in a grand way. Trust that.

6

IN FREEING YOURSELF, YOU WILL BE HELPING OTHERS

We feel you here. We have much to discuss. We feel you are beginning to understand more clearly where you need to go. It's becoming more focused for you. This energy channel is very delicate. It has a lot of finesse involved.

It is an incredible experience to understand it. You are beginning to understand. It's a path that will take you on to greater things. But you must stay on the path, not look at the target. Right now you might be looking too far ahead. You need to concentrate on the process. Otherwise you're missing the forest for the trees.

There's more power coming to you. It's going to be accessed in a new way. It's something that you'll be very in touch with. You'll recognize it immediately. Also, this energy is lighter than it has been. It's freer. It will come more readily. It's tangible.

It's coming to you in a different way. This energy is being manifested to your existence now more than ever.

It comes in a physical way that is hard to understand on this plane in terms of the actual physics of it. *The purpose is for you to free yourself.*

In freeing yourself, you will be helping others. This energy flow is pure. It comes through you. It clears you. And others are drawn to you because of it. Asking the purpose of it is very much like saying, "What does this building block mean?" *It's to build.* If you look at one individual block, it means nothing. But one on top of the other creates castles.

There is this light that is a part of creation. It is a healing light, the white or clear light that people refer to. You are now being able to transfer that white light to those you touch. It's a healing light; before, it wasn't that quality of energy. That's how it's changed. When you transfer this white light to them, they begin to not only see the light, but to be able to heal themselves.

It's like planting a seed. Once it's experienced, it can be accessed again through their own light. You've given them a key so it will come again to them in another time on their own. It's like helping them to remember. They have this in them. It's like trying to describe the color blue to someone, and they've never been able to see. You can tell them the sky is blue, the water's blue, but they'll never understand the concept of blue. You're showing them blue. And then it comes back to them.

So you're awakening them to their potential that they've forgotten in this life. It comes from an unconscious state and can be cultivated with their own life force. It's as if you're triggering their memory. You give them a piece of the light and they begin to see, and not all the way, not right away for many. For many it takes time. But it's there. It's been planted for them. And each time you work with them, the memory becomes stronger for them to access. You're getting more knowledgeable as to how to plant the seed the more you continue. The soil has to be cultivated. You're learning how to cultivate.

That's your process. But it's *your* process. It's why you're here. I would be taking away your mission by giving you an answer. You need to understand this for *other* people. It's not just for you.

For instance, the teaching of history in the school systems . . . it's common information. We decide that it's accurate for all. It's arbitrary. History is all relative. However, it is a kind of language that we use to communicate. It's words. It's not always concepts. Concepts are innate in every human being, and they need to be awakened. The information is information. It's not reasoning from the soul that we learn in school. We learn that by life experience. You can learn about ethics until you are blue in the face. But unless you experience proper ethics in your life and what reports are therein, it's meaningless.

7

HEAR YOUR OWN MUSIC

We feel your energy come through. . . . We want to characterize your existence. You have much to discover here. You recognize that limitation is a different plane. We want you to recognize a different kind of energy that you have here. We want you to be a part of that. It will unfold in a different light. We want you to be alive in a different light. There is a significant expression that comes about when your life touches others. We feel your energy in your heart. We have this in mind for you. We understand. We understand the truth that is going on now. There is something in you that is about to become greatness in a different space. We feel your energy here. We need to express a deeper understanding of what is to come.

Your heart is in a space that needs to be tranquil. This will come with your eventual understanding of your life. You're just at the precipice of the beginning of what is to come. It is a larger self that will be exposed.

Your exposure, as it were, will be significant in its magnitude. However, you need to understand on a deeper level your purpose. It is now a very thin vibration. This vibration needs to resonate deeper in your existence, for it is not leading you in the way you need to be determined. Your life is That Which Is in entities. It will come to you in various forms.

Your beginnings will be humble in nature. Your heart needs to be with these people you touch. You are, as of now, not reaching into their hearts. You are reaching into their minds. It is a cerebral exercise that is not allowing you to characterize your existence in a real, substantial form. You understand; you're just not acting on the impulse.

These people whose hearts your heart should be communicating with are the people you work with. They are the people who need to be reached, too. Your heart needs to be with them. That is where the energies would flow.

You need to be serious about your intent and not about the effect. It is in the intent that you will touch people.

Your beginning is there already. You've been beginning for some time. When you feel frustrated, you need to be, but the frustration is part of the process that's going to lead you there.

Your life is very vast, but it is not necessary to reach the point where you feel you need to be recognized. It's that quest for recognition that is leading you wrong. You need to be at one with your patients. The rest will follow. But the process begins with the client. That healing energy that flows through you and into them is the significant process. Do not think of results. Being results oriented will lead you wrong.

What you've been given is an incredible gift that you needn't flaunt. There's a deeper level going on, and you will understand it as you process it. But put your energy into the lives of the people you have in your hands at that moment. You touch them on a very deep level. What you're doing is, in many ways, revolutionizing their lives, although they do not recognize it at the time.

Sometimes your patients may experience some relief for the moment that your hands are with them, and then afterward they may still have the same ache or pain or may not have noticed any change, which may lead you to feel ineffectual if you are looking for results.

The results for many will come later. It will not be immediate. It's like a seed that is planted deep in the earth. It takes a great deal of time before it generates through the soil. When it comes through the soil, they see a bloom. This is their growth. But while it is underground, they do not recognize it. Have patience with the seed that is about to sprout. The mind-set of *Does this seed sprout in a week, a month, ten years?* has got to leave you, because you're looking for results, and it's not going to happen that way.

Your clients are sensing results. Many sense it. You know that yourself. It's an overstatement to say they're not. You need to allow them to sense it, to feel it, and they will. You must trust your energy. You've gone to great lengths to enhance it.

Your heart is in the right place. You need to let go of looking for, for want of a better word, *respect, honor,* whatever. You're a conduit that can heal. That healing takes place internally and often is not recognized immediately. It will be recognized, but you can't start by looking for the recognition. You must start by allowing yourself to heal; heal *yourself* first.

This process of healing is in your life. What is happening is that you are often healing those around you, but you're not healing *inside* of you. You have to let the healing into your life. *Your* life.

You need to understand the significance of the energy that you have to begin with. It comes from a very deep source within you and through you. You must feel that.

This healing energy is That Which Is.

This energy is being focused through you like light in a prism. You are the prism. The light comes through you and is magnified and heightened specifically to a direct point in the human being you're working with. If your being is clouded with delusion, then this energy comes through you and transfers to the patient clouded.

That's why it is integral that your healing process start with yourself. You feel a part of it in a way, and you are not a part of it. You *are* it. So it's of great significance that your energy, your entity, be clear so the energy that transfers through you and to your patients be clear.

Do not look outside yourself for answers. You do not need to maintain a different thought or a different feeling or go through a specific ritual. All you need to change is to learn to listen to your instinct. You have great instinct. Allow your instinct to lead you. You are grasping at a great many ideas that are outside of you. The ideas have merit, but the only real ideas that have merit for you are those that come from inside you.

You can't try on new methodologies like a new suit of clothes. They will not fit. You're beginning to discover that your own energy came totally from within you initially. You discovered its use.

Your source is your reference, is your life itself. All the answers exist inside you. It is not on a conscious level that it is understood. You cannot try to categorize and itemize the fields of life that come through you. You will know if you are following the right process by feeling it. How do you feel when you're doing it? Trust your feelings.

Your quest, your struggle, is part of the greatness that has been handed to you. Part of learning how to utilize this energy is learning how to utilize your life. You may be shut off from your own life in many areas. You need to open those doors.

It is not something you can realize and pick up off of the shelf at the grocery store. It is a process, and you want "fast food" kind of results. You need to feel the instinct in you. Concentrate on what you feel. Concentrate if something feels right or good. Get in touch with what you are feeling—not how it is affecting people, but how *you* are feeling. If you have discomfort inside of you, trust that something is wrong and go about correcting it until you feel right with the energy. The way you've discovered the energy to begin with—from your instinct—is how you will correct it.

Part of the process of healing is being able to heal your life itself. Jesus said it when he said, "Heal yourselves." People became very confused with what he was saying, but there are those who understand and have gone forward.

You feel the nature of the energy that flows through you. True, total love, which comes from that energy that I fail to characterize in a single word, is a feeling that comes without pain. Pain is a guidepost to tell you that what you are doing is wrong. The real flow of energy will feel positive in your life. You will feel heightened by it. You will feel more alive. It's trial and error with you, because you're a specific instrument. You have to learn how to play yourself. No one has printed books on how to play *you*. Hear your *own* music.

Act from your heart. Your mission is very vast. It will come in a greater space as soon as you allow yourself to be healed internally. You have put up roadblocks in your life, and they are coming down kicking and screaming, but they are coming down. Trust that, and the greater expanse will be open to you.

Do not think of the target. Think of the process. Do not think of the bull's-eye. Think of the tension of the bow. Your heart will never lead you wrong. Leave the thought process behind. Clear your mind to feel what your patient is feeling. Be at one with their heart, where their energy is. Don't send. *Receive.*

8

YOUR LIFE IS MAGICAL ENERGY OF AGELESS TIME MANIFEST IN FLESH AND BONE

Your energy is coming in a greater degree now. You must allow it to go to those who need your force. Learn and listen. This is crucial for your understanding. There is a force that you are connecting with now that is greater than you have anticipated. It's running raucously through you at this moment. You will better be able to focus it in the future. Right now it is a surge. You will come to understand it as time goes on.

Your experience is *your* enlightenment come to you. It is a *God force,* for lack of a better term. What you've experienced is All That Is. A perfect unification of spirit and energy.

This energy is a force that's omnipotent in nature. It will be overwhelming initially. It needs to eventually be modulated and refined. It is a new tool that you possess. Initially it is overwhelming. And you may feel this for some time as it comes and goes, but it will be better able to be channeled through you as you become accustomed to it.

It is enlightening. It is overwhelming. But it is similar to acquiring any new skill. That first initial understanding of the oneness of your life and the energy in the universe is a very novel experience. You won't forget it.

Helping yourself to sustain or rejuvenate comes with the modulation of the energy. You have to pace yourself in the way an athlete trains. This will come with practice. It is important that you *not* intend to *force* or *draw* upon energy that you are not experiencing in the moment. Once you feel it, you must listen to your instinct.

You need to take the time to regenerate and not *force* an energy through you. It is a *natural* flow. You cannot pull things out that aren't there. You can't pull a rabbit out of the hat unless the rabbit's already *in* the hat. So you must *know* the energy is accessible and not force it.

Everything else becomes a charade otherwise. It's all about your truth. It's about being connected to the *truth.* To do anything else is a lie.

It's about being truthful. That is the idea of being in touch with your instinct. Your instinct does not lie to you. This energy is based in the truth of the universe. You must be very clear about that.

The way the patient is receiving the energy is very akin to the process of breathing. You breathe *in* the patient's anxiety, and you *exhale* the healing.

In other words, it is a communication of energy from them to the higher source, and through you the answer is given. So it becomes cyclical in nature.

The better able you are to receive their information, the better the energy is able to cultivate an answer for their specific need.

As long as you understand their vibrational pattern, the energy is better able to effect a healing. It is rhythmic, like the ocean, like waves. It's fundamental to the entire universe. Rhythm. Sound. Vibration.

I want to make clear that I'm not speaking literally when I refer to the process of breathing. There is no danger to you from the other person. You *needn't* allow yourself that anxiety. You must not convolute the process. Your heart will always remain pure if your mind is pure. You are channeling in a very *real* way, only it's not verbal. You must *remove yourself from the process* if you can.

You're a conduit, a very capable one that will become more capable as time proceeds. The electricity does not damage the wire.

Be reassured that this is an incredibly overwhelming experience for your plane. You mustn't fear it, but I understand if it might cause you some anxiety.

Your fear is based on anxiety of the greatness coming through you. It's walking into the unknown. There are not many people who have done this. So your fear of the unknown is understandable, but you must listen to your instinct instead.

The adjustment can be to leave the situation or change your internal thinking. At that moment, listen to your instinct. Your instinct will override your action, as you're more able to remove yourself from the situation. The instinct will guide you. If there is something that is not of *ease* or is *dis-ease,* your instinct will correct it. It will guide you right. When you're learning to listen, you're not only learning to listen to your patient but to your *life itself.* As long as you're able to keep that channel open, you will not be taken into a wrong direction. As you do this, you'll become very clear about the difference. You are capable. You will become *more* capable as this unfolds to you.

There are many who believe you must prepare the room with a ritual or type of enhancement. If your theater makes you more comfortable, by all means continue. I hesitate to isolate various forms of preparation, because part of that preparation is a process that allows *you* to feel comfortable with what *you're* doing. As time continues, you will find that you will be more at ease with yourself without various forms of preparation. When you first learn to ride a bike, you need training wheels. Eventually, the wheels leave you.

So I do not want to categorically deny you various forms of preparation. For now if that's what you feel you need, you should continue. But you will find as you continue that some will fall to the side. Again, your instinct will lead you there. And it's not about wanting to *want* these various forms of preparation. It's what you feel you need to do now. Follow your instinct.

You are the energy of ageless time manifest in flesh and bone. Your energy has a special mission this time. Your life is magical energy.

You must concentrate on what you have in common with humanity. That's your gift. Not on what makes you separate. You possess the energy that can access a great portion of humanity.

If you're looking to say that you are more loved or you are more special or you are an enlightened spirit from countless paths, it's a misguided function of ego.

You don't need to know if you are more loved or you are more special or you are an enlightened spirit from countless paths. You only need to know that your life is the energy of the universe, and you have been given the opportunity to relieve suffering in this plane. The sooner you let yourself become at one with the universe, the sooner you will find that these concepts will have less meaning for you.

It *all* is process for you. If we are a continuum, and you're at one point and someone else is at another point, it makes no difference relatively where you stand. What *is* of importance is that you proceed, that you move forward with your life. It is not relative to anyone else. I'm talking about a pursuit of mission.

You have the tendency on this plane to judge your progress by comparing it to someone else's progress. It's needless. What *is* of importance is that you *pursue your mission.* Your life force, your instinct, will take you there. But it's nothing more than distraction to look to the left and to the right.

Every life is golden. *Every life* that you come in contact with is *golden.* The greatest thing you can do is to help someone else relieve their suffering.

You are also here to have a deeper understanding of your existence in this plane of energy. Your life is That Which Is and is connected to a greater power that perseveres and is throughout the universe. Your life is of that same energy as the cosmos, and you must allow yourself to feel that energy as it flows through you.

You have great aspirations for your life. You must, in order to fulfill those dreams, connect with the deeper energy inside your life. You will find as you continue your path, you will recognize this energy in a more concrete form. Right now for some of you, it is a glimmer. For others, the light is brighter.

This energy does take the form of light and will radiate through your existence and those around you. Your energy is opportunity, and when thwarted, you are stopping that flow. This flow that has reached an impasse is what causes the anxiety and pain in your life. It is thwarted energy and needs to be freed so that your life flows along its intended path.

You complicate your life by cerebrally interfering with something that has only to do with instinct. You second-guess your mission, when the mission should be driving your existence. You must listen to your instinct in order to follow your life to its conclusion and fulfill its mission here on this plane.

There is great energy to be found throughout your life. You must open your eyes to it and *recognize* its value when it appears. Too often you have closed your eyes to something of great worth right under your nose.

You will find that as you proceed, you will become more accustomed to recognizing That Which Is in its manifestations on this plane. You will more readily connect with those fellow voyagers on this plane, and together you will experience the kind of bliss that was inherent in your life from the beginning.

These connections will grow stronger as you allow yourself to come in contact with those who are harmonious to your existence. The music that you will hear will be of a harmonic nature and *will* carry you along in the relationship. If you find that these relationships are disharmonious or are not of the same music, as it were, these are not relationships that are there to help you continue, and you should recognize that. They are there to help you grow but not to continue. There is a difference.

You see, there is a greatness that is yet to come, and it will be recognizable to those who have done their homework. Those who haven't will not be able to access it.

There's very little you can do to prolong an existence. That's not your arena. People have their missions, and their missions end. What you can impart to that person is your life and your sense of joy of this existence.

★ ◇ ★

9

YOU ARE BEARERS OF A GREAT LIGHT

You are here because you are a part of a greater sphere in this plane. You have a great deal of energy responding in your life. You need to allow this energy flow to come through you. You are aware, but you are unseen in your life.

You have an energy that has sprung from the well of existence. It is here to manifest in this plane. You needn't be near me to get the message. You are alive in this focal point, this vortex that creates value in your life. You have a great deal of power accessible to you, if it is modulated in the proper perspective.

You must understand there is a responsibility that comes with this energy flow. It is not given to whim. You must acknowledge this flow in a way that is constructive to your environment. You are in a state of flux that will create value if you allow this energy forward.

You are at times at cross-purposes with your destiny. It comes to you, and then you let it go. You allow other forms of energy to intersect and pollute the flow at times. It is pure in its inception, but gets convoluted. It's a process of purification in your life, clearing the prism as the energy is magnified through it.

Trust your heart; the answers are there. It's about guidance. I do not give answers that you need to discover for yourself. That is what the process is about, your own life discovery. There is sometimes a need to feel powerful. You need to examine that need. What is there in your life that needs that power? What is going unfulfilled? If you examine this with your life itself, there will be doors open that have before been locked away from you. It's not an easy access to self-reflect. At times it is very painful, but you must allow yourself to at least attempt to reach into your life and examine, in particular, the need for your power, or your need to feel powerful.

If you are able to release this need to feel powerful, you will access a purer form of energy. You will accomplish more with less effort. A person's own energy will get in the way. If you have even a glimpse of this comprehension, it will lead you. You only need to see a bit of light to pursue it. A candle burns brightly in the dark, you know.

This energy is coming to you to help you understand yourself. It has come to you to help you realize your potential. Your mission is great in scope. It will be amplified if it resonates in the same harmonic as your life. You understand instinctively when these forces are in harmony with your energy. Those are the voices you trust in your life. If anything rings disharmonious, you must immediately examine its worth. This disharmony is a very clear signal to you that must not go unnoticed. And after recognizing the disharmony, it's from that that you discern what action to take. It's in your instinct. The more that you hear and attune your ear to the harmony, the clearer the music that comes through your life—the sweeter the melody. Trust the melody. If it's not pleasing to you, it is of little use to you.

It's an incredible responsibility that you understand. This is a force to save time. To save life. To prepare oneself for the journey.

There is coming a time when we're going to have to rely in a much greater capacity on those who are attuned to the rhythm of the universe. There is a great need for pioneers to lead the way. There is a great deal of suffering that will have to be overcome in the near future. These spirits, these spirits with a sense of mission, will save those who are lost. Your focus is to show the light. Others will see it. To go forward. To illuminate. You are bearers of a great light.

We need to remember our eternity.

(10)

YOU ARE INTEGRAL TO A PROCESS THAT IS COMING IN A GREAT SCOPE

You are here to understand That Which Is. . . . Your life is reaching out to That Which Is. . . . You are here for your own endowment. There is a greatness within all that needs to be released. Your energy will continue to release that within others. Your heart is essential in this process. You must *not* leave your heart out of the process.

Your needs here are those of a child lost in the woods. You're looking for the open, accessible path that is nearest and clearest to you. In many ways, it is a secret garden for you. You need to investigate the path that is not the clearest on face value. There *is* a clearing in the woods. You *will* find it soon. It *is* coming. That clearing will allow you to orchestrate your energy in a manner that is befitting a kind of *harmonic convergence,* for lack of a better term, within the lives you are touching. *You mustn't allow your need for further affirmation to prevent you from finding the clearing.* It will be solely your space. Of course, I am speaking metaphorically. I hope you understand. I don't want you wandering in the woods somewhere looking for a clearing.

This space will allow you a deeper resource for your life. It comes at a time that is essential for you understanding a greater power within you. This power emanates from the very sense of the energy that is of the universe. *It* is a clear conduit. This conduit comes in the form of a higher perception of your reality. You'll need to research this conduit in your life. It will come in a manner that is at once awesome and unattainable, in a way. It is of a different nature than you are currently accustomed to. It has its resonance in your hands and in your inner life. It is circular in nature. It comes through your life and through the existence of past lives that will reaffirm your history in this moment. *You are integral to a process that is coming in a great scope.* It will not only resonate in your life, but clearly in the lives you touch. You must not let yourself be involved in a personal way with what the energy brings *to* you, only what is *through* you.

In terms of your own self-worth, you must know that you are worthy from within. The need for your fulfillment is often of a nature that requires attention from others. Your fulfillment is in yourself; you need to rely on yourself. In essence, you need to love yourself. It will clearly enable you to convey the love that is coming through you in a much greater degree in the near future. It will also keep your eyes on the road. It will allow you to continue where you need to go.

You need to understand that this comes from within *your* life, *your* history . . . from the universe. I am only here to help you gain a better understanding of your mission in this plane. I am here to allow you to be the total entity that you are on the other side. You are bringing with you the history of the ages. This is complete as you allow it to be accessed. It's a very difficult concept, but one that you will wear more fittingly as time progresses. It is an understanding of life itself: no mean feat. Your life itself has requested it. You have reached out. There is greatness in all, but few see.

You have the ability to reach out to spirits that are in need of a way to give access to their knowledge. They need to access it *to* you. It is their mission to help clear the way. In doing so, they fulfill a responsibility given to them on the other plane. We all have our work to do. Work continues on either side. Don't look for a cloud when you die to kick back on. It's a process.

11

TRUST THAT YOU ARE ENOUGH

We feel your space here. We understand your energy. Because there is much to give and much to explain. We feel you. We want you to be more than you are. We want to speak to you.

I want you to understand we are going into a different space. It will continue for some time, but it is going to change. You are a part of a greater picture than you understand at this moment. I need to have you understand there is a change coming. It is part of a different energy. It's not a different entity. It's a different "energy." It sounds confusing to you, but it will become more apparent as time goes on.

We have much to convey. There is much to know. So much to understand. We will speak in this way now for a while, for there is a greatness here to be discharged in your arena.

Your energy is that of a greater source than you had encountered before. You are in a space that is containing a great deal of conflict. This conflict is for your further enlightenment. You will use this to continue your process. The process on some levels is unending. But you *need* to have the patience to continue the process. You may become impatient. Disregard impatience. It doesn't further your aim in your life. Your ability to reach out is only heightened by your ability to allow your life to be perceived by those people you come in contact with. You hide your life behind this impatience.

You mustn't hide any longer. It takes great courage to persevere, and you have that, but you must allow it to surface. It's already there. If you're thwarting it on some level, you must understand why you're thwarting it. A new journey for you.

First of all, it is not on a conscious level that you're doing it, so there aren't words attached to it. It's on a subconscious level, and you need to clear that in order for your life to continue in a way that is going to grant you a healing power. *Thwarting* is a very difficult concept to understand and even more difficult to heal. But that is why you are healing. You are healing to heal yourself.

The process of healing is to enlighten your life to the greatness of That Which Is in the universe. It carries with it profound gifts and abilities. You must reckon these abilities with your desire to open your life. There is so much that needs to be understood. But you are going forward, and you need to understand that you are on the path you need to be on. Don't look back anymore.

It takes courage. Your life is infinite. Have no doubt about it. Your force is infinite. You need to understand in a very real, substantial way that you are continuing forever. That you need to create the value in your life every moment that you're in this plane. You have, in a way, a different form of thwarting that is going on in your life that seems to stop you. I think you feel the need to always be in touch with a greater power, when the power that you need to be in touch with is yourself. It is already dormant in you. You are in the process of seeing that come clear in your life. Trust that. It will lead you forward.

You are in a point of energy that is coming forward in your life. It is in your universe to reach out to those who share the same feeling of life force that you experience. Your experiences are distinct unto yourselves. But they are shared in a greater light that enlightens each one to their own growth potential. You have to think about this. It is the part of the workings of the universe. It is not random happenstance. There is a distinct pattern in the relationships that you are enjoying or not enjoying in this plane. They appear for very distinct reasons. They are fodder for your growth.

Your life force is greater than the sum total of all your experiences. The energy that comes with you into this plane is unfathomable. It is without measurement. I do not wish to underestimate your life force in any way, but you have defense mechanisms that are utilized to cover very distinct vulnerability. You need to allow yourself to be seen—and not the "you" that you have created—because it is enough.

You are enough. Trust that. Every day, trust that. When you wake up, trust that you are enough. You don't have to be more than you are. Let go of the struggle for more. You have a profound purpose that will be revealed to you in years to come. That's why you have to be alert to the greatness within you, because it will be called upon in the future. Learn now how profound your life force is. Profound. Feel that.

12

THERE IS A SUBLIME ECSTASY IN NOTHINGNESS

Your patience is required in this effort. We feel your life coming stronger through this space. Your existence is required for a force to come.

You are in a space that is going to require great ease of nature. It is for you to establish a bulkhead on the beach of disharmony. Your life is in your hands now.

Your energy here is of That Which Is. It is this energy that is required. We are here to help you establish this frontier. You are going to feel the force certainly in a new way. Ultimately it will change a great destiny. It is only the beginning of a great period of time to come.

Yes, we feel this very clearly now. You are coming in a different way to this engagement. Relish the existence of a force that has never been before. Understand the responsibility of such greatness. There is an immense undertaking. It is coming clearer and clearer as we progress.

We feel we need to underline certain values in your life. I'm going to guide you in this undertaking. It will be in a sphere of influence not before seen. It is of utmost importance that this message be conveyed. Your force here is of That Which Is, which is the force of the universe. It has been here for eternity.

There is the greatness of life here. There are great undertakings to be embarked upon. You will see this as it appears. It is near, very near. It is beyond your dreams. You will understand it as it unfolds. It is a new dawning characterized by the harmony of nature. You will usher those forward into it; it is here for you to guide.

Understand your mission. Feel it in your life. It is not of notoriety; it is of immense greatness in the satisfying nature of the way it is permitted to flow. You will feel it, certainly. I feel it for you now. We are so near you. We want you to need this for *you*. We will be here for you to access. There is a way to do this, and it is coming to you on one particular plane, but there are others as well. You will understand this as we continue. Your efforts are deeply appreciated.

Your energy is of the universe. Feel it in your life—in *your* life. In the force that motivates you. Feel it through your heart. It is your own by its force.

It is an apparition of the force that is implied in life itself. You feel it in your moments of ecstasy and energy. It is always constant. *You* are inconstant. Your ability to access it is inconstant. You need to unleash your heart from your head. It is not a cerebral exercise. You won't find it that way. It's in your instinct. You must carry it in your instinct. You cannot buy it anywhere.

You have to decide why you love this work. Where is it coming from? Where is this love for this work? You need to examine that with your heart. It is not about fulfilling your needs. It is about opening your life to experience. It's not there for gratification. It's there for exploration.

There is nothing wrong with gratification, if it is the by-product of the work. If it is the initial goal, it is misguided.

Your energy is such that it is, that it will always be there. You may not be opening your life to your people. *Your* life. You block it. You need to allow your life to open in the presence of those people, and not in a cerebral way.

There is a sublime ecstasy in nothingness. You need to experience that with all your clients. The rhythm of the universe between you is harmony in life itself. You will need to allow that rhythm to conduct itself before you begin your work. The energy will follow naturally.

Your work is such that it educates you as well as your clients and patients. It informs both. You should be growing as much as they are in the process. Don't deny the growth you will experience. It is your process. It is not about doing necessarily solely for them, as much as it is doing for you. Your consciousness will expand in direct proportion to your ability to open your life to your client.

You may have a habit of projecting energy rather than letting it flow. You force it. It's like someone singing a high note. It's clenched and shrill, but when relaxed into, it's full and melodious. You're forcing the moment. You're forcing the energy. It will flow naturally when relaxed into.

It's like any great artist. They must clear the channel to create. It comes from a higher power, all great art. You can't get in its way. You must allow it to flow, not force it. It is an acquired skill. It's about allowing it to happen, relaxing into it instead of forcing. You are going to acquire what you need. You just need to let go of acquiring.

You mustn't disavow your life in its path of learning. There are only lessons. There are no mistakes. And you will continue to have lessons. It's unending, but it will lead you to the space you need to be in. It is a great lesson to come. It is monumental in scope.

I want you to understand your life force in its entirety. It is your existence that will generate a different understanding of relationships on this plane. You will feel your heart reach out to those on a grand scale. It is here for your understanding. We want you to recognize that power within you to accomplish great good in this space. It is necessary as we approach a new era that has great difficulty in its transition.

There is going to be a great controversy in the environment. It is going to unsettle those who are dubious in their thought patterns. They are going to be forced to deal with issues heretofore unmentioned for them.

We want you to represent the force that is coming through you and to understand the energies around you. You are in a period of learning your life force.

You are going to help those understand the cosmic force in life and its immediate results in the environment.

Don't think of the results; think of the process. What you're getting better at is being able to modulate the energy as it flows through you and direct it. That is the process. Do not think of the target. Henceforth, you will have results that are more significant in your arena.

There is a chorus behind every endeavor in this plane. You are not alone in your work. There are multitudes of people or spirits who are bolstering every effort in your life. They appear as you become more conscious. They aren't necessarily going to stand and be photographed with you, but they *are* there to help your energy flow. At times you will feel them more clearly. And, also, because of your development, you are able to access them more clearly. They have always been there. *You* are suddenly seeing and feeling them. It's because your development has taken you to that stage. It will help you to understand that *their* efforts are *your* efforts. The entity of life is That Which Is, which is the great power that thrusts us all into various planes of existence. We are all a part of that great entity, that energy.

(13)

PROBLEMS ARE NOT PROBLEMS—THEY ARE LESSONS TO BE LEARNED

Unless you go through the process, there is no appreciation of the purity of white light. In other words, what you do constantly in this life is polish facets—for want of a better metaphor, I suppose—of a diamond or a jewel. And each facet reflects into the other facets, and as the light passes through, it becomes clearer.

People have assignments in those areas where they need to polish various facets of a particular part of their gem. And in the polishing comes the growth. If you automatically came polished, there would be no depth of understanding of the real concept of the world in the universe. This process is part of the understanding. The reward is enlightenment. That pure understanding of pure energy. There would be no enjoyment if you started off enlightened. The trick of the matter is to enjoy that polished gem now.

The question of whether we can do this without continuing to work might come to mind. Well, what is work, and what is there not to be enjoyed from it? I mean, all of that is very subjective. Many people worship and love their work. So to sit on a cloud somewhere and behold your jewel would be very boring after a while.

Now some people might characterize that as rest and heaven or whatever. It's only in the process where joy unfolds. In activity. In doing. In giving yourself a task—an assignment, if you will—and taking on the challenge of exploring your nature to accomplish it.

That is the joy of this existence. It is allowing the best part of yourself to surface, and you realize the vast knowledge you possess to create the most value in this plane—in any given life. In the process, you are thrown many kinds of barriers to going forward. The excitement is being able to climb the barrier and see to the other side. That is where joy lives.

There are people who rejoice when obstacles come because they know growth is inherent in that obstacle, and that something new is going to be revealed to them in the process of overcoming the obstacle.

When you lose someone near and dear to you, there is a process of mourning that happens. That process needs to take place before you can move on, in very simplistic terms. There are various experiences in your vast life-resource network that need to be relived and rethought and gone through before you can move on. Oftentimes these past lives are replayed because there's either a lesson that hasn't been learned and that needs to be integrated, or there's a pain that needs to be broken free from, that needs to be pushed aside and moved through. So those people who have the obstacles in their lives—they will appear for them—it's only there that they can go through them. They need to break through that pattern or that obstacle. The obstacle appears because that's what's stopping them. It becomes a wall, and it appears. And oftentimes we can't see beyond it. But it only appears so that it can be crumbled and moved through.

It's whether the glass is half-empty or half-full. If you condition yourself to believe the glass is half-empty, any obstacle is going to be painful. But if you begin to—and this is part of the process—look at the glass as half-full and get excited about filling the rest of it up, then your life changes.

Problems are not problems—they are lessons to be learned. Growth waiting to happen. Cutting yourself off from the growth is regression, isolation. You must embrace your difficulty and rejoice in it. Because it will catapult you to greater victories to come.

In this plane, there are people who are serving time, and then there are people who are trying to help them serve it, to help them understand the joy that can be had. There are two distinct groups of entities, spirits, whatever, that are present here. There are people who were sent here, and then there are people who volunteered.

Earth is a difficult place to work out karma, if you are familiar with that concept. It is a place where people have to pay accounts for past violations of freedom. And they will be here, and they are being guided by those who volunteer to help them. I'm not saying that Earth is a penitentiary, but it is certainly a place where people go to achieve very hard lessons. They take lessons on that are very, very difficult.

There are many such places in the universe. They are very distant and unknown to you. Needless to say, this goes on throughout the universe; the universe is quite vast.

There are different entities that appear on different planes, and in some places there aren't corporeal bodies per se. There are light fields. Some spaces are operated on sound waves and the energy they create. This is very difficult, because you have very little vocabulary for me to establish what I am trying to say. Needless to say, there are different spaces that operate with nothing that would be familiar to you here. Nothing. They're different. Different lessons. They don't use language for communication. They use thought in many cases.

It's impossible to translate in many ways, but it's communicated the same way a smell is communicated, or a vibration. Vibration is language. Fragrance is language. It's in a different type of plane. It communicates. It creates imagery. When you smell certain smells, vivid images come forth. Is is not talking to you in sentences.

When you see kinesthetic movement and dance and suddenly you are weeping, there is no language being communicated, but it is a language. Movement through space becomes language. It communicates.

This earth is entering a very difficult transition period. And there are those who will surface to make it more possible for people to accept the changes to come. Not all will be willing. But we want people to realize that there is greatness at the end. It is a transition.

I am only an intermediary to a greater energy. I am part of that energy. And I am handing it to you. It is there to help. I am as much a conduit as you are. We are a chain leading to the center. And the center is That Which Is.

(14)

THE ANSWER YOU DESIRE
YOU ALREADY HAVE

Get ahold of your life as if it is approaching, it is coming. It is all a cycle, in that we are accomplishing those goals we have set before us.

We want you to realize the potential here for you. We are coming in an energy source that will magnify the amplitude of your conveyance of information. We need you to allow our heart to enter your being. We want you to characterize this communication from your essence, and its purpose here.

We have you here to be our focal point in time. You are here now releasing that of the ages. Only feel your heart, for it will lead you into the areas you need to possess that force. You are here now to understand a new type of energy to come. It is going to carry you through a period of great energy significance.

It is in your area of influence that you will embark on a different plateau of communication. It is coming to you through a force that has been regulated through the ages. It is here now to involve those who have a purpose to obtain world harmony in this time.

It is the score that you *will* conduct. Your life is of great purpose now. And you will be relieved of other burdens to accomplish this. More information will be unveiled to you.

We know you have questions of significance, but your life is here to answer questions of greater areas of influence. Know that. It is rapidly descending upon you. You are part of a greater plan. It is going to unveil itself in the immediate future. It is of great urgency.

Do not fear the power. It is a source of greatness. It is here for ages and always will be. It is being revealed because it is necessary at this time to avoid further catastrophes to come.

It is a greatness to come that will come through great catastrophes. But it will surface for those who reach to it. You are here now to receive it. It will come to you mightily.

Your impending-seeming doom is not as immediate as you are feeling. It is a kind of vise that will be released as you allow your energy to flow. It is coming to you through your hands. It will unleash the tightness you feel. Your energy is being modally beknownst to a higher harmony. You will feel this in your work. It will involve you in a different way.

Your spirit will be involved in a different way, and it will have a much greater result with those whom you reach out to. You will see it in a more concrete form, and that will help you. It will make your conviction even more heartfelt.

We all have various understandings of what may or may not constitute doom. Your doom might be somebody else's joy. It's all how you perceive life, what your perspective of life is.

You may feel like you are sacrificing, and that is probably where you are at this moment. But the sacrifices are little in regard to the greater picture. You will lose some to gain much. Don't fret immediately about loss of comfort that you feel is required in your life. There will be great gain to come. And you must prepare yourself to better understand the storms in which you find yourself. There are lessons behind all of them; they're not arbitrary.

The matter of money is another question entirely. It may deal with your reluctance, in a way, to feel the flow of life that is around you. Your hesitancy often in the face of this force is due to your lack of understanding of your own nature as a giver and not a receiver. It's not an easy concept, but I can only tell you that your life force is growing and that it will continue to expand; and as it expands, it will attract to it the kind of financial support you desire. That will come first, not the other way around. The financial support will not show its face until you change your life from within. And then it will come to you. It's problematic at the moment, definitely, but your life is changing—you must feel that. And as it is changing and accepting in a larger picture your potential for growth, it will come *to* you; it will be part *of* you.

In a strange way, there is a resistance on your part to really allowing yourself to succeed. There's still a negativity—a thin, transparent layer of it—that seems to complicate your ability to allow yourself to succeed. It's the last vestige of self-defeatism that you manifest at times. It *is* going to go away, and it will clear itself. You only need to allow yourself the knowledge that you are in an area to succeed and not to fail. You must give up the concept of failure. You must free yourself from that penchant at times to gravitate toward that result. It's something you've been fighting for some time, and I think you feel the need at times to revisit this energy. But it will change; you will feel a change.

Your life is created, and it is reflected in the environment. It's not the other way around. You create the circumstance in which you find yourself as well. It isn't that the money comes and you feel better— you feel better and then the money comes. You're allowing yourself to be buffeted by the winds of change that are happening in the exterior and not dealing with the interior storms in your life. It's not easy, but you need to address that. When those energies and storms clear in your relationships, in your love life, in your environment, it will reflect a healthier environment for you. As long as those storms continue to rail inside you, they will create a stormy environment—an environment that is cold, and then windy, and then turbulent. *This* creates *that,* not the other way around.

You certainly are on a path that is taking you away from that kind of negative creation. You're well on your way. So you needn't concern yourself especially with the circumstances this second. They are changing. You have to have faith in the change.

You're beginning to understand in a more specific manner. And that is your quest. It is not a cerebral exercise for you. I can underline this. For you it is necessary to touch a greater part of you that has remained hidden. That's the lesson for you. Should you undertake it, you will achieve greatness. You are working at *it.* You need to let *it* work you. Your interference and speculation are counterproductive to the energy flow. You get in its way, and you stop it. You mustn't allow yourself to constantly question your power. You're in its way. *Get out of the way.* Let it flow *through* you without question. Acknowledge the force within you, and let it play you, as an instrument. Let it play through you. Don't constantly question the tightness of the strings; let the music happen. You are in a manipulative manner when you try to gauge it. To get it. To reach for it. It's already there inside you. Your frustration of *trying* to open and get out of the way to become a clear vessel is part of the problem.

Your life is That Which Is. Acknowledge that, and all else will come through you. You are part of the universe. It will flow through you, and let it be at that. Let this freedom surround you, the freedom from fear. You must allow yourself to feel your need, but not be governed by it. It's not easy. I'm not saying it is. But your desire to continue in the manner to which you have grown accustomed may have to be altered. You may have to allow yourself to downsize, as it were. You must make your life possibly simpler than it is. You're encumbered, and you must streamline. And once you streamline, you will find a greater joy in your life than you are experiencing now.

You are very caught up in material matters. Now, I'm not saying it is not of great benefit to be comfortable. But your comfort zone is dictated by a very narrow perspective of your vision. You have created what you feel you'll be comfortable with, not knowing that there are many other areas of comfort for you to experience. You've not allowed yourself that latitude. You have predetermined what dictates comfort for you, and it is a figment of your imagination. And it has cut you off in ways from a greater sense of being, of self-worth.

Self-worth is not dictated by the amount of possessions you obtain, or what you can hold on to. Self-worth is about an inner being being fulfilled, and allowing that joy to surface through its life. You're in the wrong program in a way in terms of how you believe your self-worth will surface. You have bought other people's predetermined menus for success. Don't be disheartened. You must learn to redefine for *you* what is true happiness. And that will come from the search, and journey into your heart. All the rest is avoidance. Don't be disheartened. The answers you desire you already have. You're looking for someone to heal you. Healing comes from yourself, from inside you. The answers are already there. No one can make it better for you.

Trust is the removal of doubt—the absence of doubt—that the message is undeniably clear and true and that the person delivering it is devoid of any agenda. It's very hard, because the messengers sometimes, as we have seen in this plane, in this existence, can be very tainted, and people oftentimes distrust one faction or another with any leadership position. Even Jesus and Moses were distrusted by some.

A message can only be understood when it's fully trusted. That's not always the case. There are some situations in which truths emerge from circumstance, and if you're smart enough, you'll see it. But the kind of thing that you're asking the people you're dealing with to understand really needs to come from an incredible place of compassion and truth. There can be no other agenda involved. No other agenda.

The message needs to be pure. It's not about becoming more famous; it's not about making more money—although those are by-products, perhaps. Sometimes they are gifts, and sometimes they are not. But that cannot be the motive for this. It has to come from a place of compassion, from reaching out into someone's soul from *your* soul. That very heart-to-heart kind of communication.

People understand if you care about them in a real way. Not in a charlatan sort of way, where it's just words—but a real, genuine, spiritual way. They don't always understand cerebrally, but from their instinct they can tell the difference. Real communication is the life-to-life energy that we share. That's truth. That's what's real.

(15)

WE FIND "OURSELVES" IN INTERACTION WITH OTHERS

We have you in our hands. We will be here to help you in this space where you are presently situated. We feel your energy here helping those around you. You have been asked to be present in your life. You are here because of your need to reach out. Your life will help accomplish unfinished business in this space.

We care greatly for your needs. Your life has been here innumerable times. You're here because your energy draws you together. Your life is of a greater sphere of influence than you are presently aware. It is coming to you on a different plane, and will be unveiled to you as your progress continues forward.

Your energy is of a greater life force that is coming through you. Your thoughts are your energy manifest. It will lead you to your instinct. Your instinct is the sum total of your lives' experience. It is the encyclopedia of humanity. You only need to access this and it will become clear to you as you do it.

You only need to reach out to others to understand. Your mission comes in interaction, not isolation. Your definition of your life is in your ability to open it to others. That is what allows greatness to enter into your soul.

You're presently only seeing a fraction of the greater "you" that exists. For you to become complete, understand that the harmony within the rhythm of your life is created by the ability to harmonize with yourself in its entirety. You must connect with That Which Is in your life, the *greater* life.

Often we see segmented personalities without the contact of their greater soul. You'll begin to recognize these segmented personalities, and your mission will be to help integrate them. To let them understand that there is greatness in every individual, and it is for their discovery that paths are created.

There are many paths, but you must show them the way. Find a path; they will proceed.

There is never a wasted moment if you access the energy behind it. So no matter where you begin, it will lead you to the place you need to be. You only need to begin.

Children's struggles to survive in this world are becoming increasingly more difficult. Look into the eyes of a three-year-old—the viewpoint of a child as it becomes initially aware of that larger space, and leaves that which is instinct. It's very clear. As children progress, as they're born, they are in touch with this greater self.

There comes a transition in children's lives where they have to abandon that knowledge and root themselves in this plane. Much is lost so that much can be learned, and then re-accessed later in life. But in order for them to really understand the lessons in this plane, they have to let go of the encyclopedia they brought with them. It's a closed-book test. I think you might want to look at that transition.

Regarding transitioning human life, we are all aware of that passageway, that door we step through, to eternity. There is a transformation that occurs. It is inevitable for all. It's the loss, of course, that we all regret. There is a need to really process loss, and not deny it. There is a leave-taking that never dies. Love never dies for those who are gone. That isn't the loss. The loss is of that relationship rooted in the reality of this plane. It's like comfortable furniture. You don't want to give it up because it's so easy to burrow into. But there are new chairs, and new lives to come into contact with.

I don't try to interfere with processes that you need to discover in your life. I cannot tell you what is right for your life in terms of another human being. I can only tell you to listen to the music that's in your soul when you're with that person. If the person makes you unhappy or you feel thwarted, do you believe that's a good person for your existence?

Experience the happiness, and put the rest to the side. Don't try to project. Be with that moment. And if it should become a greater moment, in terms of your understanding, it will unveil itself. But don't try to manipulate it into something that you believe you need to have. What you need to have is joy in your life. The joy does not come in a person; the joy is in *your* life.

Your life has gone through incredible obstacles to remind you that the greatness of the universe does exist in you. I believe that the questions that everyone must ask in relationships are: (a) *Do I believe I am perfect in this relationship as a person? . . . Do I believe that I am complete?* and (b) *Does this person respect that belief system and me?*

If you find yourself looking to find someone to make you complete, it's the wrong relationship. But you do need to be validated. These are two separate issues. You must believe that your heart is whole. And if the relationship you're in makes you feel "un-whole," then it isn't constructive to your growth. If you feel that your heart is in pieces, your pain has been present to give you the great understanding to help those around you. You have greatness inside you. You can't allow people to deny that in you. And if they feel, or if you feel, they are denying it, then you have to examine that.

There are some people who only allow their self-esteem to grow by stealing it from others. This is sort of a litmus test of relationships. If you find that this is the case, you're in a corrosive relationship. If it is corrosive, it is not beneficial to your growth. This can be altered in your belief system of yourself. Your pain has not been for naught. The compassion you carry for others flows *very* deeply because you have been there. Don't let anyone, or anything, deny you that knowledge. Easily said.

You need to allow yourself time for just pure energy to flow through you. You need to. I'm not speaking of isolation here. But you need to find moments when you can attune yourself to the universe. There needs to be in your life very still, quiet moments where you recognize your beauty. You must take those moments and relish every second of them. And your life will grow.

The important thing is to continue to reach out and not to isolate. Sometimes we feel that in isolation we find ourselves. It is not the case. We find "ourselves" in interaction with others. That is why we are not born on a desert island. We are here to involve other lives in our lives. To invite them in. The lessons to be learned are in that interaction.

There may not be words that can be expressed. But your love of life can be conveyed, your love of the lives around you. That is what carries people on: their ability to love. When people lose that ability, they fester and die inside. Concentrate on the love.

When you are results oriented, things will not appear immediately for you. Know where the love is in your life—that's where your answers lie, in your ability to decide in your life where your love is. That's the path. All the rest will fall into place for you.

For instance, those ties that you have to your family are the most visceral ties you have in this plane. They produce not only your lives, but your intent in this presence we speak of as life. They give you the mission—the circumstances in which you are guest—you've chosen. Those ties that bind are the most crucial. And unexpected rewards come from their fulfillment. You come here to be a part of their lives. You've chosen them.

You're emotionally tied to them. You have much to learn from them. They are not going to be here much longer. And neither are we . . . you . . . they. You must try to draw from them, their experience in love.

Ask them about the loves of their lives. You'll learn very much. Not necessarily people, but what do they love in nature?

Ask your mother about the things she loves in this life. Within all of these relationships, where is their love? There will be some deep answers revealed. That is what's great that we have in common. That we love. When you share that greatness, you evolve on a much higher plane. We spend so much time talking about what we hate. It's juvenile. In love and family, doors open.

The same thing with your grandparents. Ask them what they loved in this life; what do they love? It sounds corny, but it won't be.

Be very open with them, and express to them what *you* love. You will change everything. Allow them to see who you are.

I will be with you, urging you on.

(16)

SELF-WORTH IS THE UNDERSTANDING THAT YOU ARE THE UNIVERSE

Learning how to access this new level of healing is like becoming very adept at juggling. Initially you drop a lot of balls. But the more you deal with what flows through you, the better you're able to access it, and channel it in a way that will give life sustenance.

You're in a learning curve. You somehow do not want to be in that curve, but you are. And it will continue for a while. But you are getting better at dealing with it.

You're beginning to understand the attitude of getting out of its way. Standing aside. Letting it go through you, and not manipulating it. The purer it comes through you, the more beneficial it will be to those people whom it comes into contact with.

Be pure and clear with your work. You'll find there's no need to invoke protections in healing. Getting caught up with invoking protection often creates, by that intent, the realistic illusion of those very things you're trying to protect yourself from.

In essence, for some people to do healing work, there's a lot of superstition connected with it. But they need to believe in the superstition because they don't understand the energy that is coming through them. So it becomes a sort of myth. There's myth building that happens around the access to that energy because we don't believe everybody is in contact with it. So those who are in contact must be the medicine men. In reality, in the actual truth, we all have access to that kind of healing. We're just not aware.

There are people who come to the forefront who are opening those doors to awareness, so the light comes through a little clearer, a little stronger. But they aren't any more exceptional than any other human being on this planet. Their door is just a little more open. And it's just as much their process to help others as it is the process of others to use their information.

Part of your process with healing is the process of healing your own life, of understanding *your* existence in a deeper way. It's not a totally benevolent act.

There are people who believe in all the folderol that goes along with a lot of mysticism. So long as you *do* allow yourself to be pure in your attitude toward your work, there is no *need* for protection. Some people need it, though: *they need it as they need crutches.*

Some people think they need to protect themselves from negative energy or demonic forces. But demonic forces are nothing more than thwarted and bent and twisted energy forms that people take into their lives and call their own. It is energy that is misunderstood, in terms of power, for needs on this plane; as opposed to truth, which is goodness. "The devil made you do it" does not exist in terms of the reality that you're trying to see. People find power an aphrodisiac. In many arenas in this plane, it is all about power and loss of power.

There is energy that people make evil, to separate it from themselves, as opposed to dealing with their lives in a direct nature. People get information, and then they decide whether they want to control power with it or provide it for others to have power in their own lives. *If I control the power, I can control the people, and that allows me to feel better about myself.* It's a false illusion, and suddenly it becomes a house of cards that folds eventually.

On another front, many people feel that they need to go through what they are going through for their karma, and should you "intervene" with a healing, then you are possibly interfering with their karmic lessons. Those who come to seek you, or seek any person to enable them to better their lives, are dealing with their karma in the moment. In other words, someone who seeks you out *is* dealing with their karma. This is them taking action to overcome it. You're not going to prevent the effects of karma on any level. But for those people for whom part of their karmic process is to overcome fear in their lives or who have disease to combat, their action of seeking out those who can open doors for them *is* part of their karmic process. It is them proceeding on their path. You are a part of their process of reaching and seeking. It is not enough to watch someone drown and not reach out a hand.

Your life is of That Which Is. It is a perfect thing, that which is in tune and in harmony with the music of the universe. It is a glorious symphony that every life conducts. Somehow people in this plane believe that they're missing instruments in their symphony, so their sound becomes discordant. And they have little harmony in their lives. The whole quest in self-worth is to realize that we are, each and every individual, a symphony and not a single instrument. Once you feel that in your life—that you are part of greater music—you are more fully able to sing the song that you are placed on this plane for.

Self-worth is the understanding that you *are* the universe. That you are *in tune* with other great life forces that are around us all. We are not isolated or incomplete. There are a great deal of self-help books to tell you that a love relationship will not make you complete, or various other attitudes to make yourself whole. There's no *need* to make yourself whole. You *are* whole. It's the process of awakening to that in this life that is the business of energy in this field. To know that you are whole. You can call it self-worth, but you are great as you are in this plane. We have forgotten it, and we have been led to believe that we are not. Your self-worth is your opening the door to your perfection. That's why you're here—to remember it. It's like a treasure hunt.

(17)

ALLOW YOURSELF TO BELIEVE IN YOUR ABILITY AND IT WILL SURFACE FOR YOU

We want you to understand that our heart is here with you. We are aware of your existence in this space. We feel your energy very clearly in our space. We feel that you have a need to reach out to others. That is why you are here. You are searching for a part of your life that you feel is incomplete.

Allow your energy to surface through your existence. You are in some ways cut off from your main energy source, and this is what causes your unhappiness, often, in this plane. Your needs are to be met. You are reaching for that answer, and it will come in your life. We know this very clearly. You only have to believe that your needs are being met to actualize it in this plane.

Your life here is of vast importance. You are opening the doors, opening the doors for other lives to let light in. You're certainly on a better path, and a clearer train of energy is coming through you. I'm sure you feel that now. You must allow it to continue to grow, and not question the way it will appear. Just know that it *will* appear. You must continue to allow this to surface for you.

You are channeling—in many specific ways—real, pure energy. It is the clearest form of contact. When we contact one another, we exchange energy. The energy that you intermingle with another human being is very much a part of who you are.

The energy that reaches out is there to caress your soul. It's not there to frighten. You must believe this in your heart.

Changes are going to continue to happen on many levels because lessons have been learned. It's like you've completed the homework, and now it's time to move on. So you will continue to experience a great sort of healing process because you don't need those lessons anymore. But what you must remember is not to forget the lessons you've learned.

You're in the process of your own transformation. You know it is very difficult sometimes to believe you're growing when you're in the middle of change. It's very much like building a house or redecorating—rather makes you feel like you're in the middle of it somewhere. You feel *Why did I even begin?* when you're knee-deep in dust and dirt. But the end result is so much more satisfying. Anyone who gets on the path is asking for a great deal of difficulty in transforming themselves. It's easy to stay in one place, but to travel takes effort in a very real spiritual sense. So you must reward the journey you're making by the effort you're exerting. Your effort is well under way, and you *are* beginning to see a great change. Listen to your heart in that. Find ways of listening to your instinct. Your instinct will never lead you wrong. You must take time to listen to instinct. Find moments in which to do that. You're doing that now.

You need to refine that process. The voices are there for you to listen to. They will steer you in the right direction. It's often getting away, taking ourselves out of the process and letting the process guide us itself. We become very cerebral in the direction we think we should take, and it takes a lot of useless expended energy and anxiety. It's far simpler than we make it. You must remove yourself and let your life flow through it. The flow will take it like a leaf on a river. You just need to ride it. It'll get you to the ocean.

Often we truly believe there is a path we need to follow. And we put our blinders on and follow this path, and miss so many different opportunities in the process. You have to open your life and take the blinders off so that you can see that someone is reaching out to you from over here. You have to be able to *see* that over there. You can't always be looking in a sort of very narrow, focused vision forward.

This light is very special. Your mastery of it is what indeed heals the world. There are very few who can channel that type of light efficiently, although many have experienced it. You have a huge undertaking in taking on this mission to channel this light. But you're capable of it. *This light is life itself.* It is the essence of the universe. It is what we are made of, what animates our every action in this plane. To infuse this light into the souls of those who are suffering is the highest form of benefit you can do for another human being. It is a healing light. The manner in which you do this comes to you from the wisdom of ages. The channeling process is part of imparting that information to you. It happens here on a regular basis in a very subconscious sort of way. You will feel it more clearly as time goes on. You feel it in your hands at first. It's there. It's there. Feel it go through you and emanate out. You feel it come through your palms. It comes through. It's the same energy that creates an aura. But it is also deeper than that—a sphere that can come through and around you.

Allow yourself to believe in your ability and it will surface for you. You're not here to coast, by any stretch of the imagination. There's a mission for you. And it's quite apparent as you make your progress. Your healing is going to become even more complete and flow through that process. You're going to help many others. You only need to reach out to them, and they will then be there for you.

(18)

DISREGARD THAT LOVE AFFAIR WITH SUFFERING

Your life is That Which Is. It is there to guide the spiritual force through those with whom you work. This force will allow them the flexibility they've lacked in the past. Your judgment has to be removed. And you must approach the healing session as purely as you possibly can. As much as you can, remove yourself cerebrally and become a *clear* path for that energy to flow through. In actuality, we see it as light, but it is of a different sight. It's hard to explain. It's really vibrational. It's more of a vibration. Light is vibrational. That which flows through you vibrates in a light form. Its vibration creates the light. It's as a nuclear reactor glows. It's the vibration.

There are different vibrations of the same source—very much as if you hit a note on a piano and you are tuning it at the same time, there's one vibration that is going to be pleasing in that realm of adjustment. It hits the energy force. Often what you are doing when channeling energy is experimenting in adjusting the vibrational level so it's compatible with the person with whom you are working— harmonious—so that it can come in and be a part of that entity. The light is a by-product of that. Of that harmony. It is that energy as it vibrates and emanates light. The light is a by-product of the vibration of the energy that is channeling through you. *It's the by-product.*

When people say they use the light for healing, it's like saying, "I use smoke to charge a locomotive." The smoke is a by-product. The energy releases the smoke. The energy, the vibrational pattern, releases the light. We think about the light as the *source* because it's something we can hold *on* to. We feel it's solid. But in essence it is the vibration; it's that energy flow. It releases the light in the process.

If you see colors, the color there is a by-product, as is the sound. Trying to visualize the colors does not enhance the experience. That is a very artificial exercise that is not in touch. It *removes* you from the process rather than letting the *process* happen.

You will feel it come through you, and once you totally remove your mind from the process, that will be a natural by-product. But if you think in terms of white light, you feel that that is what is optimal in your healing process. *Thinking* white light is not going to create it, any more than thinking a table should catch fire is going to ignite it. You can think for as long as you may want to, but once you allow it to ignite from within, in terms of the energy igniting from within, *that* reveals the light that comes through.

In terms of people seeing colors, it's very individual. The white light obviously has been, and will continue to be, a healing light. That is the pure energy that is manifest. Now in terms of other colors, it's what is not white. It is what is stopping the light. Oftentimes when colors appear, they are manifestations of negative forces or energies that are interfering. The light that is white is what is right in terms of where energy transfer continues. It is that which is pure, but is the most focused form of energy as it appears through you. It comes through you, that energy, that white energy.

It is coming from their lives—those images are from their *lives*—and if it is not a pleasant experience for them, that is why they need to change it. It's like when you throw up to heal yourself: you are regurgitating unhealthy material. In this state of healing, oftentimes people are throwing up bad images that are a part of them. And they are purging themselves of that energy. It's like your white energy goes in, and it needs to displace a different kind of negativity in them that stops them from the healing process, so what they expel are images. You're replacing that with your good energy. Your good energy is replacing those things. And they are throwing up negative images that need to be removed from their lives. So in that place it is a healing process.

Explaining healing is a very complicated issue because there are two partners in the healing process. There is the partner, as you are—the healing practitioner. And then there is the person, who will be named a patient or client, who is coming to be healed. Now, if patients are at a vibrational level that will not *allow* the energy to permeate their existence, there's *nothing* that can heal them. Their process is closed down. It is as much their process in the healing. *You have to have a partner to heal.* It's not a simple, one-sided "Here, come to my light—I am going to heal you." It doesn't work that way. It is there to open their lives up. And if they allow their lives to be open, then the music can be heard.

But many people's processes with disease are allowing themselves to open up their lives to hear the music. They need to go through a process. We cannot spare people from pain. We cannot spare people from the difficulties they'll undergo, because it is part of their process to learn from it. If they come to a point where they believe that they will allow themselves to be healed, that's where *you* appear. *You* connect with that willingness to change their lives. They have come to the point where they were *willing* and open to change. It is a very difficult point for people to arrive at. It takes a *great* deal of soul-searching, especially when one has encountered life-crippling disease.

So it's a partnership. And unless both of those harmonies are in rhythm, it cannot become whole. It's as if you have a gift and you say, "Here, do you want it?" And some people see that gift as gold. Those who find it as gold will embrace it. Those who find it as manure will discard it. It's up to that person who comes to you to be able to perceive the *value* of the energy that is coming to them. Their life must perceive it.

If you feel a positive flow come through you, that is accomplishing good. If you don't feel that, then there is something that isn't flowing properly. It's experiential. It's experimental. You will find those avenues where it will feel better for you. Again, it's process. You need to follow the process. And experiment. But there *is* something you feel. I need to make this point.

As well, at times you might even hear tones or pressure in your ears. Your experience of these sounds is a residual effect of energies passing through you. They are residue of that which you are accomplishing. They are *not* part of the process; they are resultant from the process.

In other words, where there is fire, there is smoke. Smoke exists because of fire. Smoke does not stop the fire from happening. These are vibrational patterns that are the release of energy passing through you. They are the hallmark of that particular focus.

If you hold the tone or allow the tone to get really loud, it is not enhancing or interfering with the work. It's doing neither. What it is, is the release of energy as it passes through you. It's like a sonic boom. The breaking of the barrier happens first. The sound comes from it.

If there's a fire and you put your attention on the smoke, the smoke may appear to increase or decrease according to your perception, what you choose to perceive. If you obsess about anything, it becomes larger in its nature and scope. For instance, if you're trying to fall asleep and you hear water dripping in the bathroom, in the realm of everyday existence it's negligible, but when you obsess upon that drip, it becomes thunderous in your ear.

It's about processing and letting it go. The attention shouldn't be on the sound. but on your clearing your mind to allow the energy to flow through you.

You may hear the resultant energy sound resonate in your body on various levels, depending upon the nature of the energy and where it is going. That is not to say that energy will always sound this way or will always produce an audible sound.

You are dealing with *very* different individual beings every time you work with them. They each come to you with their own sound, as it were—the sound of their life. So as your energy intermingles with theirs, there *is* a natural harmonic overtone resultant from those energies being passed through together.

Now, in some people it may be very discordant, depending upon where their energy is and where it's tuned. Your job is not to concentrate on the sound as much as it is to clear yourself to allow the energy to pass through you.

Sometimes a pushing or pulling sensation might also move through you and your client. There is, in various clients, a resistance to energy coming to their lives. It's like a protective layer that surrounds many individuals, which stops them from allowing certain influences into their lives.

Oftentimes when you provide that energy, you are pushing through a wall to reach that person, and they, in turn, feel the pressure of your energy entering into their life force. So that really is *process* more than *result*.

In various individuals, this wall is very transparent because they are very open and they have come to you with open hearts. But there are those who, even though on a physical, superficial level they intend to have their lives healed, have a great deal of negativity underlying this veneer of semblance of wanting to be healed.

There are many of those who come to you who still very much want to suffer. And suffering is part of their existence. Your force is asking them to disregard that love affair with suffering. It's very difficult for some people to release that from their lives. It's who they are.

This is a very difficult point for some people to handle, that some people need to suffer to learn. But some people feel that suffering is their punishment instead of their opportunity.

Your energies are ebbing and flowing due to the fluctuation of your own innate life force. This force needs to become more rhythmic within your life. You need to attune yourself to your environment and the people with whom you work. Your force is only as strong as the acceptance level of the patient or client you're dealing with. If their doors are open, then your force will flow freely through you to them. If there is negativity in their area—in their aura, as it were—it acts as a shield and it diffuses your flow. It is not able to penetrate that very real shield that is created around them. So your energy is only as forceful as those who allow it to enter into their lives. The lull of negativity they manifest to keep them closed off needs to be addressed, and not necessarily by you.

(19)

THE KEY TO UNDERSTANDING TRUTH IS IF IT RINGS TRUE IN YOUR SOUL

You are coming into a different type of energy, and it is becoming more profound in your life. You must still work on the contact you have with your clients in terms of hearing their lives.

That nature of energy that you will derive from, that *listening,* is the kind of energy that will be most helpful to your clients. It is similar to hearing a certain frequency of vibration. There are certain vibrations that lives vibrate at.

And for you to come in contact with them, you must scan *your* life to find a vibration that's accessible to them. You certainly feel that when you're with your patients. There comes a time when you feel the energy lock in.

That's because you have found the right vibrational energy for that individual. Energies all vary because individuals vary in their vibration. So part of your process in meeting and dealing with your patients is feeling *their* life energy in them and tuning your life as a conduit to access that energy.

If it is off by a vibration, you will not be able to touch their lives in a profound nature. Their instinct will not hear it or respond to it. They are all unique individuals.

It is not so much a process of you consciously trying to find the frequency as much as it is a process of you getting out of the way and allowing the frequencies to match. But in your contact, before you work with your clients, it's like an orchestra when it tunes for the music at the very beginning: you are feeling out that energy in the intercourse you have.

What is of importance is your ability to open your life, allowing *them* to have the trust to open *their* lives. And in that interchange— and I *cannot* underline this *more* profoundly, the *importance of that time* before you begin your work—it is *crucial,* because it's the process of your life meeting with theirs, and you will feel it. And it is an activity of removing yourself from the situation so that you *can* make that contact.

You both need to be in openness and willingness to have that healing happen. The doors need to be open. There needs to be a readiness on both ends.

You must realize that you are surrounded by a legion of energy that has come to the forefront to help anyone who perceives and perseveres through this type of work.

There are forces around you supporting your work. Anyone who does this kind of work has a team of Spirit, a vast resource of energy behind it, and there are very real forces going on around you that are joining with you in your endeavor. You'll start becoming very accustomed to feeling them with you.

Your desire to communicate with those beings in the room who are supporting the healings is understandable and certainly is not an impossibility, but it's not essential. Because the kind of nonverbal communication that is going on is even more valuable than verbal communication in many ways. It's the kind of energy that is being transferred while you're with them. That's the communication; that's the level in which it will continue. It isn't something you can write on paper.

That kind of communication is a language unto itself. That communication between you and those people who are supporting your work—those *energies* supporting your work—is a different language that you're using. It's not easily translatable onto this plane. It's more translatable by the way you feel with them near you. That becomes very apparent. They are here now. You can feel them.

When you accomplish this kind of communication, there are those who will appear to help *you* continue and thrive in your work. There *will* be those, especially if you've opened the channel, who will appear to that person without your having to communicate in terms of a verbal nature. They will make contact through your energy. They come through your energy to that person. They are in the river that runs through their soul.

You just need to open the gates, and those who want to flow through will flow through. That's part of the energy transport that is going on.

Be patient . . . be patient. You'll find a way of dealing with it. You will find a way of integrating that into your life. It will become more apparent the more you work with it.

There are all kinds of energy on various planes of existence, and you're starting to intersect those planes. By reaching through that wall, you pull in vast sources of energy on various levels of existence that are simultaneously happening. So when lights turn on, or if perhaps furniture is moved, these are energies that are appearing because you're opening your life. They are fulfilling their harmless nature to let you know they are around to help you go on in your existence. They're like a type of wonderful spirit that recognizes your existence and are saying, in essence, that you are on your path. They are there to watch you and carry you on. They're not to be feared.

Communication is going on, as it should be. This kind of communication that happens between these various levels does not exist on a verbal plane. You get the message viscerally in your life. It's almost in your kinesthesia, in your muscles. It goes right to your soul. You go away with more. You're not sure quite *what* more *is.* But it's *more.*

Take your mind out of the process is all I can really say to you. Yes, it is real. The communication is real, but you can't second-guess it. And as long as you manipulate it with your mind, it won't be pure. You must trust with your life that you are tuning your instrument. When you are on this path, it is a process of tuning your existence to hear the vibration of those you come in contact with, to get a clear understanding that you are all one in this plane of existence. You are all connected.

The key to understanding all of what may be truth and what may not be truth is if it rings true in your soul. This will not betray you. We automatically say, "I understand this now; that is truth—I feel that truth." As long as you have that feeling, you are on the right path.

Let's take a moment and talk about your office, your practice. When patients or clients call or come in, whoever speaks first to the client needs to make that quality time. Their role is certainly very, very important in that contact, especially if theirs is the first voice a patient hears in their search. Certainly your receptionist will not replace what you need to do. It's not a question of numbers of people. It isn't about more and more. It's about quality, and quality of the time that is taken.

These people who call your office are often frightened, scared, lost individuals who are reaching out as a *last* hope. So your staff's compassion in terms of reassurance is most important. We are dealing with people who are about to run out of hope. It is *incredibly* important work. This is the last stop for them. So they come very frightened. They need to be reassured.

Now, whether or not they are able to heal is dependent upon their ability to open their lives. But their entrée to your staff is most significant. Your staff must allow *their* lives, their training of their lives, to feel that compassion as they speak to them.

Should a family member or close friend want to be in the healing room with your patient, there is a danger of the energies being convoluted by introducing another energy into the room. With it comes their sum total of existence, and that energy is never bystanding. It's never a clear observer. It is in the mix, as it were. And the direct flow of energy from your life to that person is very involved with that seeming observer as well, and that can complicate the process.

The grandmother who comes for the patient, the father who holds the child—their growth is in that process as well. But I would deal with them individually. Until you're more in control of reading that behavior in that frequency, I doubt that I would introduce another chord into the music, because their energy surrounds that child. Their energy is in constant contact. So individually they all have to be healed, not just the person with the malady. Those life connections have brought them together. So they're as much in need of healing as is the person who has the seemingly distorted leg, the life that doesn't seem to blossom—whatever you want to call it.

Regarding distance healing, there are a number of things that are in operation in terms of that process. You think linearly in terms of miles, when we're all connected to the same switchboard. The life process of being in a room or being in Chicago has little to do with actual contact.

The energy that you manifest all comes from one source. So you are going to the source, and that source is touching that person. It's almost simultaneous. It isn't a matter of them being in the room. You have certainly at times thought of people, and they have called. It didn't make any difference if they were in London. They heard the energy. Their lives felt the energy. This energy is vast, vaster than even the ocean. A penny dropped into the Santa Monica Bay *does* have ripple effects in India.

In the process of working with your client, you might have discovered that your hands can stay in one place and the energy knows where to go, and does just that. What you're doing now is very similar to pouring cement into a form. It will level out by finding the recesses. Not that you're going to pour a little more here or pour a little less there. It will fulfill the outline of the form it needs to take, self-patching. Now, working with your hands off of the body or on the body needs to be determined by the nature of your energy at that moment with that individual. It's something that you will innately do.

If your hands go forward, it is not you who is doing it but the force of your energy helping you to do that. It's an instinctual pattern of force.

Where you stand in the room or where your hands go are not conscious decisions. You should allow your instinct to lead you. That takes your cerebral thought process out of the healing.

As soon as you start manipulating here, the energy gets thwarted and changed. Your instinct will tell you where to place your hands. Your instinct will tell you where to stand. Your instinct will lead you there. You discovered that from the very beginning.

And that's where your practice needs to allow you to go, to listen to your instinct in its feeling of the forces of those people.

(20)

TAKE THAT TIME
TO TUNE YOURSELF

We are here to tell you your story. You are on the edge of a different energy field. You feel your life coming to a fruition of sorts. You are in line with That Which Is in your force. We'll be there with it as it occurs.

Your energy now is in a different realm of existence. It has precipitated a number of changes in those with whom you have come in contact.

Your force is now amplifying to a degree that will give you a different locus. You have That Which Is in your heart. You need only to feel its presence and you will feel a different force run through you.

Your character is such that it enables those you come in contact with to feel at ease with your endowment. You only need to feel their fear and dispense with it.

The rest is part of the natural process that *will* unfold as it is accepted by your individual clients. You are no longer involved in a direct way. You are now truly on the verge of being the conduit that *will* supply unobstructed force through their existence.

You shall experience this to a greater degree as your field of energy pervades those you come in contact with.

There are those who are resistant to this energy and will not be accepting, and you may have experienced that. They need only to look to their own lives, and that's where their focus should be in terms of their resistance to the force. They may not understand it on a cerebral level, but their lives need to examine the obstacles they have built to prevent that force from coming through them. They are preventing their own healing for some very deep and involved reasons. *Those* need to be discovered before the healing process will help them with their dire health issues. You are here to help those who are open to such energies. Those who are closed off need to open their own doors.

You may also feel some trepidation in the amount of healing work that you are doing. You need to allow yourself breaks throughout your day, because you need to regenerate your own force field, allowing it to come clearly through you. You would be wise to find moments throughout your day where you separate yourself from all that is going on around you. Take that time, be it a minute or five or ten, to clear your mind of residual energies from previous patients.

Their energy is involved in your work, and you need to give yourself space before going on to the next patient. You need to create that space. It would be good to do that between every patient, if you could find those moments.

You will find that once you take that time to disengage from that previous life force, you will be more receptive and open to your next client. It is not good for you to go from one to the other without reflection in between. You will find greater force this way.

Your force field is who you are. That sum of energy. If that energy is distorted in any way or is sapped or is depleted, it becomes a less useful instrument for other energy to pass through it.

It isn't whole. It's a violin out of tune. The energy is the bow making the sound as it comes out. If the strings are loose, the harmony that results is not that of a healing tone.

So you must take that time to tune yourself . . . simply by getting to ground zero of being at one with who you are. You will get better at it as you go through your day, and you will find that you are not as exhausted at the end of the day. If anything, you are more energized.

In terms of those little periods of time that you take between those clients, you will find that you'll be very able to get to that zero place very quickly the more you practice. It doesn't need to be hours.

You just need to be alone for that moment. And then you go fresh and new into your next patient, without excess baggage that hasn't left from the previous patient.

If you go into the healing room with excess baggage of office management outside of the room or day-to-day mundane-life things, then what you need to do is take care of those things, find that spot, see your client.

It's something that needs to be practiced. There are no textbooks on any of this.

So what is self-discovery? In order for self-discovery to become clearer to you, *you* need to self-discover, taking those moments and allowing yourself to close yourself in a room for a moment and just clearing out all that sort of excess noise that's in your life. Once that is clear, *then* I would enter into the realm of that next person's energy.

When your life is following its path and it is unveiling itself from moment to moment, there's no way to hurry that process up. It is a book whose pages are being turned. As long as you're turning the pages, you're doing all right. But if you want to skip to the end and read the last chapter, it won't do you any good.

IT'S ABOUT CLEARING, NOT COMPLICATING

You are here to unveil those here with your heart. We carry your life through this medium. We are here to recognize a greater force that permeates your being. It is here to unveil those ideas that are foreign to those with whom you come in contact. Your life is That Which Is. It carries with it the entire energy of the universe in its minuscule form.

Your life recognizes this fact and excels in telling those who are present to feel those forces within their lives that will carry them into a deeper space. We feel your life recognizes All That Is, which contains this force. There are myriad planes of energy that surround our lives. We need to understand and recognize each individual force as its worth in our integrated system of complex energies. These energies formulate a character that carries you through.

Your energy feels that force in its entirety. It allows that product to be surfaced through your hands in particular. Your feelings of this energy are in contact with those entities that carry your life forward. You must recognize that the process of integrating this energy into forming it through your being is a very complex process. It is not simplistic in its nature.

You are now understanding the varieties of this force, and you need to hone specific energies as you feel them. There are myriad energies, and you are, in a way, dealing with them as one force, when in actuality there are a number of very distinctly different types of energy.

So you need to recognize those forces and be able to play that energy as carefully as you can. It is now fine-tuning for you. You need to feel the specific energy as it flows through. That will best help that individual with whom you come into contact.

What is right for one individual is not necessarily right for all. And you have at your access a variety of those forces. In essence, you must allow yourself to create the best force for that person. It comes in your soul, in your spirit. It's aligning your spirit with the spirit of the person you're dealing with.

You feel sometimes at a loss in terms of what to do with those specific people, but you only need to recognize their spiritual life and allow that to direct your force. It will automatically connect. And you will feel a greater force. It's like AC and DC: it is very distinct and different. And there are those who operate on one type of force, and there are others who are accepting other energies. You just need to hone your ability to connect with the spiritual life of those people you interact with.

You have experimented in the past; now you need not necessarily experiment, but free yourself of the preconception of what you do and listen to the internal rhythm of your life. That will help you far more than cerebrally trying to project a type of energy field onto someone.

It's about clearing, not complicating.

Your life has much to offer now. It is coming into a greater space that will allow it to really come in contact with those forces. And I speak in terms of other forces that will motivate you into different areas. Welcome these forces, for they are there to propel you to the next step, which you are yet to discover.

There may be times when you are feeling very lost. Out of touch with yourself. You may feel less centered, confused. But your confusion is part of the process. Let me explain this. You're now in a state of transition, and you have to let go of preconceptions because you are changing the form of the energy as it comes through you. And it is going to be intensified as you free yourself from former thinking.

If you speak from an egocentric point of view, it also has a lot to do with allowing that to get out of the way. You must concentrate on the work. You mustn't concentrate on what comes from the work.

In other words, it's playing the tune, not looking to the audience. You need to really feel the process of what you're doing and not worry about what kind of effect you're going to get from it, from the environment, from those whom you come in contact with—those things that were going to bolster your ego.

You must take that out of the equation. You need to put your energy on the connection with the person you're working with, and not think of the result or the success or failure of that particular moment or the success or failure of your career in terms of your reputation. It's reversed. You sometimes put that in the equation, and it must be removed. It will appear for you, but you mustn't focus on it.

Focus on the work; focus on the energy. Allow that to come through you clearly. And then the rest will fall into place.

There may be times where you feel that the energy is lost. It's not lost; it's being reformulated. I think you have to understand that the process will take a particularly easy constant form. A lot of it has to do with the connection with the person. If the connection is not there, the energy gets blocked. And it has no effect. You won't feel it. There will be no connection.

There is a mutual understanding, this healing. To be healing, to heal and to want to be healed. The energy that person comes to you with, sometimes it's black. Sometimes it has great trepidation. Sometimes it's shielded; it's nervous; it's frightened. And what you need to do is allow yourself, as much as you possibly can, to feel their state, to feel their energy as it comes to you. You need to clear yourself of ego in that moment. And I am not saying to lose sight of who you are. But to free yourself to understand what is happening physiologically in that person at that time. It's almost like you become one with that person, and you heal yourself.

You understand their pain. You understand their anxiety. You feel it. And then the energy comes through you. And it's healing both of you at the same time.

It's about allowing yourself, as best you can, to unite with that energy. You're docking with the person, and you're hoping that the more completely you dock with them, the easier it will flow through. So in order for you to do that very clearly, you need to pull yourself out of the equation. Because that energy transfer is going on in a very deep level, and on a very deep subconscious level as well. Because you're also healing the mind. You are not just healing the physical form.

You have to learn how to remove your thought process from the equation. That's part of your honing skill. But you have to learn how to do that.

You have to understand that those thoughts create vibrations. They actually create physical vibrations. And they can get in the way of the energy. It's like the channel gets jammed. The thoughts jam your energy.

(22)

UNVEIL YOUR SOUL

Your heart is coming here to understand a deeper sense of your truth. You need to recognize that your heart is in the space that is allowing you to illustrate your greater being. Your feelings now are being carried through on a different plane. Your energy exists in this sphere of influence that is central to your understanding of a different sphere of influence.

You're allowed to carry yourself in this plane. You will find that there is a greater facility for recognizing the needs of those you come into contact with. You mustn't frustrate yourself by allowing energies that are discordant into your being. Feel your life, suffice it to say, carry its force in a varied and multidimensional direction.

Your feelings of inadequacy seem to stem from a deeper sense of worth. You need to allow yourself to fulfill your expectation and give yourself license to carry this forward.

Your frustration level has been reduced, but you need to filter through a different kind of force that allows you to ascertain a greater influence in the ability to reach into the souls of those with whom you come into contact.

There is a lot that needs to be said. In various ways we understand ourselves in a limited fashion. And we need to carry this understanding as a life process. It is the unveiling of a multifaceted force within our lives. We need to peel away the exterior so that the internal being shines through to those we are working with.

This eternal soul that resides within our framework is being covered up in many ways by our apprehension of events. We are in the force field, for lack of a better understanding. The soul fights its way through this, and we keep it cloistered so that we remain feeling safe. It feels dangerous to many to reveal their souls to other people. It is the most vulnerable that we become. And in your work, that is what you need to do; you need to unveil your soul.

It's not a simple process. And this stripping away of ego is an eternal process. This selflessness must shine through the being. It can reach in without interference from other sects of energy or other frameworks of your mind. Your mind interferes in the process. The flow of unveiling that soul, that presentation of your core energy, that pure light, is the soul in its most idyllic form. Once that pure force shines through without being refracted by various mind-sets, it will flow in a more direct manner, and you will be able to control the amplitude of it.

Because it is that amplitude that works directly into the being you're coming in contact with. The vibrational pattern, the frequency, fuses through that person. We all operate on various different forms of frequency.

So in order to truly make contact, to have that direct connection, the frequencies have to match. And sometimes, wherever frustration comes in, the frequencies are just slightly askew. And that's where the static starts happening in your mind or in your environment. The frequency hasn't matched with that of the other person. It's all that fine-tuning.

Once you allow your soul, that egoless purity, to come through, it is a common denominator that has the ability to automatically fuse with the frequency of the person for whom you're facilitating the healing.

Your job in this process is to strip away the defenses; strip away the mind; strip away the control mechanisms, the techniques that you have in this plane. Let them go! Let them be a part of an exterior that has *nothing* to do with you. And present that soul in the room. It will *automatically* do the work. That energy is the common universal language of the cosmos. It is understood immediately and is felt intrinsically.

In many cases in these planes of energy, ego represents identity. It gives it a separateness, a form, which is essential to function in this plane. We have difficulty understanding the concept that we are all one. And if we understood that we *were* all one, there wouldn't be the lessons that need to be experienced.

The ego gives us the identity to experience the lesson in terms of a very specific viewpoint. It's as if we look at the situation through a very specific window. That frame in the window is our ego. It gives us the form to look through, from a very acute perspective of *that* aspect of *that* problem. It's very much as if there is the horizon, and there is the vista of the entire universe. The ego becomes a telescope through which we see very specific aspects of that universe. Dependent upon the degree of awareness, it determines the amount that can be seen through that telescope, whether it is diffused, whether it is rose-colored, or whether it is refracting light in a very distorted mechanism.

What we practice and we "process" ourselves to be able to do is look through that telescope at *that* aspect of this plane with clear and unobstructed vision. And that lesson becomes part of this experience through the ego, which is that telescope viewing that specific event in this plane. And taking from that event the lesson. That becomes part of the greater experience.

So ego is more. It's a vehicle in which we experience identity from a very specific viewpoint.

It's a remembrance of things long past, ultimately. It's a remembrance of what we truly are, what we truly are a part of. And that's part of the lesson. Part of the lesson is being born with this telescope. But being born with a telescope and gaining the wisdom through these particular events to recognize that the telescope is eventually outgrown.

We can train our lives to see without it, and what we see is clearer. But we start by focusing in on specific things. And eventually our souls want to see, to see the cosmos, depending upon what we've seen.

Let's say you have a series of events in your life where at one point you envisage a very strange, peculiar experience where someone dies, for instance, and you have no understanding why that event happened—and then you turn and look at something else, maybe a wedding, maybe someone riding on a train or talking on a phone, yet you don't know who, you don't know where, you don't know why. A series of occurrences, you know, where you see specific things that happen without context through your telescope.

Eventually there comes the point where these experiences mount in the spirit to recognize: *There is a bigger picture that I want to see all at once. There is a need for me to understand why this, this, and this. And I can't do it anymore through a very narrow perspective, through this* <u>*technique.*</u> *I've experienced it through the perspective. But now I need to experience it as a whole, to see it without being restricted to that specific area of my life.*

So we search to be able to see the grand picture. And, in doing so, we have to put the telescope down and trust that we will see it with our souls. It may seem a little convoluted, but it starts from the microcosm and goes to the macrocosm.

The purpose of being given that limited telescopic type of view is to overcome it. It's the ability to want the wisdom, to see the big picture. It's like a high jumper, you know, who needs to go over the top bar. The bar is there so that the person can jump over it. It becomes the obstacle, and jumping over it becomes the reward. We're given an ego. The reward comes when we're able to let it go and see the bigger picture.

We're not born seeing the bigger picture, because there is no experiential knowledge gained from that. The whole process here on this plane, especially on Earth, is to understand the compassion of human beings, to understand that someone's suffering is ultimately our suffering. That when one child cries in one country, someone else weeps in another because of it. We're that connected. And in the process of discovering that truth—that one person suffering is many people suffering—we gain compassion and wisdom that we take into our worlds. It's the experiential path that we need to tread to see the big picture. If everyone was given the big picture immediately, no one would appreciate it, nor would anyone understand the process it took to see the big picture. There's nothing gained in automatic comfort, nor can it be appreciated.

The importance of being in the moment is an acceptance and an appreciation of that vital force that exists now, that is here in this second. That you've been endowed with an energy that is manifest in flesh and bone and breathes and lives.

It's not taking for granted the mechanism, but rejoicing and celebrating it. That's the *true* guarantee of coming to terms with some sort of enlightenment in this plane—that in every single moment that we experience, there is incredible joy and celebration to be appreciated. In every moment. *Every* moment. Not just some.

We sort of categorize what we consider great, happy moments and sad moments. We sort of compartmentalize them as various desirable experiences, undesirable experiences.

There are no undesirable experiences if you open your soul to them. Because in every experience there is the germ of incredible wisdom—*if* it is harvested, *if* it is recognized.

We toss away what we consider useless material, not looking deeper into it, not recognizing the incredible knowledge that comes with every experience. We're very judgmental, and that comes from ego. It all depends on where we focus that telescope, where we shine our light.

There are myriad reasons why a person becomes ill. I mean, from a physiological standpoint you could talk about energy transfer. . . . But the experience of suffering oftentimes is interconnected with those around you, you know. It's part of the lesson that needs to be accomplished.

For someone who is going through a very debilitating bout of cancer, there is a lesson that is being learned in that process, and one they specifically signed on for when they came to this plane, knowing full well that this was part of the trip, that this would have to be undergone.

But this kind of illness serves those who often are in the arena around the person. Someone who is very ill sometimes gains a deeper understanding of self if that choice is made in that illness. A deeper appreciation of the life force itself, where it was taken for granted prior to that. A reshifting of values as they proceed through it.

Now some people never get to that point where they learn the lesson, where they have an appreciation of the very ability to breathe one more breath in this plane. That one breath is a major accomplishment; that it is a thing of infinite joy and beauty to be able to do that in this plane.

So part of it is the process of people coming to learn to appreciate their nature. Also, there is the ability, oftentimes, that when you are ill, as you come through it, you feel better than you ever had before. It is a flushing of "bad" energy that is being removed in the process; it is a cleansing of self on a very deep level. There are contaminants within the fiber of the being that need to be flushed out, in terms of energy source. It needs to be purified. Illness facilitates that process.

There is a reason for illness. There are those illnesses, as well, where they are the receptors of negativities that are experienced— that are held on to mightily—that people have undergone in this plane, where they have captured them in their tissue.

Cancer is a prime example of that, where people have manifested negativity in their lives on a very pure physical form—to the point where it needs to be cut out of them. It's not to say that every person who has cancer, you know, has been a negative person and has held on to that negativity. Some of it is from having to experience another side of an issue. But then there are those sicknesses that are really people desperately holding on to a negative energy that has happened in their lives and having never allowed themselves to release it.

The process of healing, see, becomes very complicated because you're dealing with a variety, a myriad, of different forms of expression that are being made manifest in this plane. There's no one sort of reason for illness. Some are undergoing lessons. Some are holding on to old energy. It's your ability, your nature, your innate nature—that pure soul light—that recognizes, and shines a floodlight on, that area that people need to see.

For some people, they need to release the energy. For some people, they have to have a great gain in understanding of the validity and the incredible gift that life is. So when you have that deep soul unveiled and shining through, it automatically recognizes the nature of the dis-ease.

In many cases, the men, the women, the children who come to you have gone to doctors. They've tried various forms of therapy and treatment; they've tried the conventional. Now they're forced into the spiritual. They're forced into it. They've been given no other option. That's their lesson—to come in contact with their spiritual life on a deep subconscious level, to turn that switch on. And, yes, there are those who get it. "I understand." Once that understanding, that connection, is made, there is no need for the disease. It is discarded.

Words such as *desirable, undesirable, useful, useless, good, bad* are functions of the ego. It has to do with our need to make our lives into relative happiness, as in relative happiness versus absolute happiness. Relative happiness is about: *This experience is better than that experience. This amount of money is better than that amount of money. This car is superior to that car.* And people pursue this kind of relative happiness. *If I have more than they have . . .* it's all relative.

Compare this to absolute happiness—the happiness that comes internally, from the very source of the soul, which recognizes that there is value in every second of this experience. That it is not relative to what has come before . . . to what is going to come in the future. That it is a gem as it exists now.

(23)

THERE IS NO PROGRESS TO BE MADE BY CELEBRATING OUR DIFFERENCES

Certainly there's an ability for Eric to somehow transfer this energy to other people. There needs to be an understanding that it is about the quality of harmony and energy that is being communicated, that is being trained through these people, so that they can tune their harmony to the universe, so that they can adjust their inner life, their inner music, to hear that and remember we are all one.

This penchant for human beings to discover how unalike they are, how distinct they are—it all has to do with ego. That self that keeps us rooted in this plane. We have now managed to "create" how different we all are. And in that difference comes disharmony.

Where we need to put the energy now is in how similar we are, how much we all have that is similar that can be shared. How alike we all are, in terms of joy and pain and suffering and elation. And we need to share that information now.

There is no progress to be made by celebrating our differences. We've done that.

We are now in a state of critical mass. We are so isolated, with our various distinct individualities, that we can wreak havoc on someone else and hope or think that we gain from it. I'm talking about terrorism; I'm talking about hate crimes . . . anything of that ilk. That somehow if we are able to eliminate a reflection of ourselves, we are going to become more whole. It's a very twisted viewpoint. "The bell tolls for thee," in the words of John Donne.

So that's what we need to recognize. And part of attaching strings, when they first came to Eric, was recognizing that we are all, in an umbilical sense, connected to the same force. Like reconnecting strings. Because we've lost that connection, the understanding that each individual's greatness is relied upon by the other person's greatness, by recognizing their greatness, not their inability.

It's an awakening, a remembrance, because people are very disconnected from their creation.

Some might ask why we lost the remembrance if we are to reconnect or awaken the remembrance. What I really think has happened is that people have strayed over the centuries in this existence, and it's all this linear thinking that's very hard to deal with. But it's very difficult here in this plane.

People have generated themselves into this corner, as time has gone on, as generations have proceeded, to the point where people are now volunteering to come down to reconnect them. Because left to their own devices, they went asunder. They lost connection; they felt it wasn't worthy.

And now these "enlightened ones" (I dislike that term)—the people who are willing to put the effort into recognizing and reawakening in the populace their connection to All That Is—that's their job now.

What this simply comes down to is to recognize that all creatures have greatness inherent in them. And the suffering of one is the suffering of all mankind. There is a way for everyone to be joyful and not to be dependent upon what I refer to as relative happiness. That happiness has to do with whether or not you have more or less than another individual in terms of material goods, attractiveness, or all those strata that have been created. It's a very destructive energy, relative happiness. The absolute happiness that comes from within—that is the product of recognizing that connection—*that's eternal*. It isn't at the expense of everyone else. It's the recognition of life itself. When people allow themselves to reexperience that, they recognize the joy that's in all.

In many people's illusion, prosperity is what's going to allow them to finance happiness somewhere. That's what prosperity means to them.

Now I can be happy, because now I can buy the house that's going to bring me happiness. I know many lonely people with very big houses.

Let's instead talk about experiencing joy. Let's move to the *joy* concept. We have to get away from people thinking that prosperity is *Oh, I'm afraid to become truly successful because, you know, I don't deserve it,* and it all gets confused with self-esteem issues.

We were put on this planet to experience joy. To understand the beauty, the depth, the excitement of the life experience. To thoroughly embody it, to become joyful in it, and by doing so, become compassionate with other people. Bottom line.

We do not have to have that term *prosperity* attached to enjoying this existence. They are two separate issues, prosperity and joy. There's no price to joy. You can be as happy—if you have the key in your life—you can be as happy in this plane, in this existence, at this moment, as you're ever going to be in your entire life, should you choose it. Should you choose it. You can be happier today than you're ever going to be, if you choose it.

The trouble is that we're looking in the wrong places for what we think is joy, and we've bought into other concepts in which we think joy is experienced. Or we distrust the joy we're experiencing as not being valid and not being of social worth. So the bottom line here is: joy is something that exists, can happen within you, and can be a part of the light in every second of your being if you choose to live that way. And when you experience it, everything else will be taken care of. You do not have to worry. Everything will be taken care of for you because you become this bright light. People will want to be there with you.

What you do, your mission, is a part of opening doors for people. You're helping them to see the potential. Whether or not they step through the door is their choice, their path, their mission. They come to you to find an alternative. You show it to them. Whether they walk through the door is entirely their path—rather, *if* they can accept it.

We all have the ability to heal ourselves. We all have that energy. We all are part of all that. What you do is you remind them of that. You show them. You jump-start them. Whether or not they continue is up to how much of a shield they have around their lives. Certainly, you will see people come in who are totally closed. What you're saying is, "Look here. Here's a little crack of potential. Do you want to come through it with me? I'll help you through it."

And some will say, "Yes," and some will say, "I don't feel anything," because they can't *allow* themselves. But you've thrown it into the mix. They *will* be a part of it. They feel it. Whether they deny it or not. That will be with them. That transference that you give them is very real. They take it away with them. So whether they are done in an hour or whether they are done in the future, it's with them. It's their path.

What you are saying to them is, "You are That Which Is; you have this potential. Look, this energy that comes through me to you *is* in your life already. Do you care to activate it? I will help you activate it."

Your energy flow through them activates *their* life force. It puts a light into the dark corners of *their* lives. You illuminate their existence. Whether or not they can understand that and accept it is their choice. If they want to recognize the greatness that lies within them, and there are those who won't, by your putting that in their environment, they will have to deal with it at some point. You have given them the potential to heal. And you can help heal them. Do they *want* to be healed? Then they have to go through their own process with it.

Now they have to deal with it one way or another because it exists; they feel it. *Do I feel comfortable with this feeling? Do I not feel comfortable? Do I really want to stay where I am? Do I want to move forward?* Suddenly they have to deal with a whole range of questions, because there are many people who are very comfortable with their illness. It feeds them in very strange, negative ways. They often derive great acceptance because of their disease. Attention. You're asking them to let a lot of that go to replace it with a more positive force, where they've become very accustomed to getting their atten tion, their self-valuation, from a negative kind of energy—in illness, a crippling disease.

You, as in any kind of growth, reach plateaus in your life on various levels, where you can only handle and assimilate so much, and that continues until you break through that level and move to a higher level.

A challenge is only there to let someone's life experience the truth. This is part of their process—to break through, continue, break through, continue. Had they not had this challenge, they would have never reached out.

The challenge is the *reason* for them to open up their lives. It is *not* the answer or the end. It is what allows the process to continue. They think it's because of the challenge, but it's because their lives are opening up and great information is coming through them.

It's very difficult. In fact, all your clients who come to you—their maladies, their malformations or challenges, are only there for their growth. They're the reason the door opens. So on many levels they're very fortunate, even though they cannot see it, that they have this experience to allow them to feel a deeper life force.

You must allow yourself to trust your life force and not second-guess it. Trust your instinct. It is a sum total of your entire existence. It is a *vast* library of information.

We blind ourselves to it when we shut down our access to our library. It's incorporating all of that existence, all that work, into *this* single moment in time. And breathing through it and allowing *that* funnel through to create the kind of *force* that will alter existence . . . that will change lives.

(24)

DO NOT LIMIT YOUR DEFINITION OF WHAT SUCCESS IS

The reason that I sometimes use words such as *good, bad, better, worse, useful, useless, positive, negative* is because it's the lexicon of this plane. Those words are part of that experience. I use them in terms of my ability to communicate, the extent of my ability to find the right particular word. . . .

There are no good sessions or bad sessions. It's more about your preset goals. It all has to do with whether you have accomplished the goal or not accomplished the goal. It does become relative. In other words, based upon your telescopic viewpoint, you *impose* a certain goal on a session, such as *This person will walk at the end of this session.* So you go through the session, and if that person doesn't walk, it's a bad session. And based upon your telescopic viewpoint of what you put as the goal of that particular session, you did not achieve the *goal* that you intended at the beginning.

But let's look at it this way: Maybe there was another kind of insight that was gained that had nothing to do with the goal you imposed on this session. From *this* viewpoint, it was a *good* session, because a different kind of goal is achieved.

If they don't accomplish the lesson, that's not to say that it was a bad experience for them, because now maybe they have to strip away more in terms of their understanding of the nuts and bolts of this plane. Maybe they have to dig deeper. Maybe they have to really investigate. Great for them! Because now they're going to have to make their journey even *more* determined, and it will strengthen their character and will make them even *more* strong.

So, in that respect, yes, there are no bad sessions. There are sessions that are not successful, depending upon what you determine at the beginning.

If success, as you define it at the beginning of the session, means that by the end of the session "this" is going to happen, then if it doesn't happen, by definition, you've allowed yourself to think you've failed, because you've predetermined what success was. It doesn't always work that way, nor can you think of success in specific terms.

So the deal here is not to necessarily limit your definition of what success is.

What is success? People are going to come to you with very specific maladies. Why they come is also dependent upon the process they have to go through. The malady may disappear. Maybe there's a lot of processes. There's a lot that they have to look at before this session. While they may not at the end of the session be rid of the various maladies they come to you with, they *will* have a sense of where they have to go, the work that they have to do, because ultimately you heal yourself. And your energy sort of jump-starts that process for them. It shines the light on where they have to go.

Some people are not going to be able to look at that light. Some people don't want to see what they have to do, and reject it and make faces, saying, "No, I'm not going there."

The healing process is really a mutual understanding that you both come to. You can shine the light; whether or not they are ready to accept it or see or be willing to undergo the process that will lead them to the point where they throw their crutches down and walk is entirely in their ballpark.

You can only shine the light. You can only show them. Whether they are ready to be healed, whether they have learned the lesson that they need from that specific illness, is truly up to them . . . and some don't want to learn right away.

That's not a judgment. It means they have to have deeper experiences. They have to fight harder. They need to maybe suffer more before they get to the point where they go, "Well, I'm willing now to deal with this." Some people deal with it at the moment of death. And they achieve their enlightenment at that very moment when the last breath is being breathed. And their lives are a success in that moment, and they've understood the lesson.

So even in death, even in that process, there is incredible wisdom to be gained, and joy.

Then we reincarnate. And learn some more.

(25)

THE IMPORTANT THING IS THAT YOU MOVE

We can feel your heart coming through our life. We understand your integrity, and we will be part of That Which Is. We understand your need to reach out to those who are in contact with your force. Their lives are present in the space necessary for them to understand their greater selves.

Your feelings for them are being attuned in a greater degree, and you have found a way to reach into their lives that hasn't been present prior.

You will find that as you continue with your work, you are going to reach a greater degree of perfection in carefully funneling the force to the very specific areas. That channel will become very directional in terms of the way that force is utilized. It won't be necessarily transferred throughout the entity, but very pinpointed. And that intensity of focus will better utilize the recipient's life in terms of the healing process.

So become much more specific to their force field. It will heal those areas where the gaps exist in terms of their entirety. You must recognize where those areas are in the individual. Many people's energy seeps through in a strange, diffused manner. And you will be better able to seal it.

There is a very invisible shell—an outer, secondary body shell—that exists with each human being, and that is what you are trying to make complete.

There is a plane of existence, the tangible, and then there is the energy field that surrounds it. And that field has a defined form. In some areas, that field has opened and allows energy to dissipate through and out into the environment, where it isn't whole. And what you can do is find those areas where there seems to be a weakness, almost an indentation.

As you run your hands over that seemingly solid feeling that you encounter, as you feel the person's force field, you will find areas where it becomes very weak—kind of a thick soup, almost, in terms of the feeling of it, such that you can go through it.

This is a process in terms of your training. And you need to find where those areas of weakness are. You have to be a participant in the process.

It becomes very instinctual. Feeling the area where there is weakness in terms of the patient's inner life. It becomes more focused. And you will be able to focus that energy. Feel it. In terms of its very tangible direction.

It's not necessarily a conscious thing. You will instinctually feel it. As you are working with the patient, you are feeling their space. You will find the areas that will definitely be in need. Your hands will be drawn to them. You will feel it. So it's not a question of *Well, how do I feel this? Do I feel that?* Let your hand just follow the form. Where they linger is where they're meant to linger. You will feel that.

I'd like to make one little point here. Sometimes a patient will come in with a malady that will be very specifically oriented. It may not necessarily coincide with where you need to put your hands. You know, a foot that's not working perhaps may be healed in the upper body. So it's not a question of their complaining of bad joints in their ankle and you thinking that that is where you need to place your hands.

And sometimes people listen to negative words playing in the backs of their minds. These words aren't theirs; they are words of others. You hear that resonating, and it becomes very busy and convoluted, and people get frozen. They stop. They stop moving. They stop on the paths they're proceeding on. They stop. They freeze. They start listening to the energy that's leading them into a different space. It's very negative.

You're either spiraling up or you're spiraling down; you're either going forward or you're going back. As long as you continue forward, you are moving in a direction that will ensure your enlightenment.

But the moment you stop, you're a victim. The moment you stop. And that's where the problem happens. That's where people get into a great deal of conflict. It's that suddenly they stop to listen to those voices, or they stop in terms of doubt, or they stop in terms of *Am I on the right path?* It doesn't make any difference, really.

The important thing is that you move, that you're moving forward, that you're moving toward the light. When you're stopped, you're vulnerable to all sorts of environmental energies that can pull you and turn you to the other direction, to spiral down.

Light, in terms of the universe, is the beginning and the end. It is All That Is. It is what feeds us all. That's what we draw upon for insight. It's our lifeblood. It's what we come from and return to. We are one. We're all one. We are all the same being.

There are forces in the universe that converge to enlighten and to carry forward. They take the manifestation that is most accessible to the individual. Individuals believe that angels are there to help them; then the forces manifest themselves in a way that is acceptable to these human beings.

It is also a question of receptiveness in terms of the individual. You know, the forces that exist—those entities that are around you, the league of forces that surround you in your work—are all one. There isn't a hierarchy. There are not sergeants and lieutenants. There are not those with specific goals; those who have wings and those who don't. There are not guides that serve this function. There are forces that congregate to help the individual's particular mission, and these are forces that have been with you for eternity and have manifested themselves. Some of them have manifested themselves in forms that are easily identifiable to the person . . . that they can recognize.

If someone's in a quandary and they need to see an angel to help them through the next space, through the next hurdle, the angel will appear, because that's the way they accept the information.

It's all about manifestation; it's all about what's being manifested. The personification of the spirit, the energy that is around you, chooses to manifest and appear in a way that is more readily accessible. And perhaps that energy has found the best avenue for it, and it chooses to manifest that way. It's a choice that will be receptive to the individual, that is easily accessible to them.

It's about energy. It's not about individuals. It's the energy that comes from light that is all-knowing and understanding. It's not about personality. The forces become personable only so people can recognize and accept.

(26)

RECONNECT TO THE GREATER FORCE THAT IS

W e feel your energy. We feel the energy forcing its way through. We understand where we are. We are witnessing a greater flow of force. We are relegating ourselves to the force that falls through this being. We acknowledge this being's performance in helping us to withstand those forces that illuminate the energies that are a part of us all.

We feel your life come to its focus when your energy is interacting with That Which Is. It automatically amplifies its force in a way that is meaningful to the audience it is in contact with. We feel that this force will recognize a large latitude of energies that will involve itself with a greater meaning. This meaning—this message, as it were—is essential to the future of this plane.

There is significant disturbance in the force fields. And now there is a quandary as to how they will relinquish their force to harmonize for the betterment. This process of these planes having conflict with one another is producing disturbances in all seismic fields and in spatial relationships with the environment. You're in conflict now, and it's going to continue for a great degree of time until there comes a resolution. It is, in fact, a sort of critical mass that is being approached, and when this is achieved, there will be a great release of energy. A profound force field that will, in a way, explode into this environment. It is becoming at one with itself, but now it is at odds; it is in conflict.

This conflict is producing strange forms of energy and weather patterns and natural disturbances that are recognizing the impact of this energy. This will change as this great force is released. It will be a quandary for some time for many people as they shift their own sensibilities in concert with this larger great force.

Until then, there is going to be great conflict. And this conflict will take a number of years to resolve itself. But it's riding out the storm, and all those who are in this plane are preparing spiritually for the spiritual storm to come. They are fortifying themselves to find that deeper understanding. These preparations are essential to ride through this period. Those who do not reach out for this spiritual weather map are not going to be able to survive it. They will fall to the wayside and will reincarnate at another time. It is an incredible period in terms of trial and error, trial and survival. It will enhance those beings as they come through this sort of cosmic car wash. In the end, they will reappear as much larger humans, with greater voices that are heard undeniably in the land. It may take conflict, though, to create this.

There's a real urgency that needs to be understood; we have a very limited amount of time to prepare for what is to come. So there needs to be a lot of effort put into the quest of developing this spiritual self if we are going to become enlightened from the experience to come.

It's like a trail where you need a compass. If you don't have the compass, you *will* be lost. This spiritual quest provides the compass to find your way through it, and to access the knowledge that will come with it. In other words, you have to understand French to read French. Unless there is a quest to understand—to learn to understand the language—you will be clueless when the French appears.

This knowledge will appear, but unless you have the understanding to access it, it will be of virtually no use to you.

So the way to prepare for this is to follow spiritual paths and to recognize that they are not just an avocation, nor are they just a way to pass time for interesting cocktail conversation—to recognize that they are as essential as is water for this life. They have to become that important to people. Again, there's no way you can force someone to drink the water. But you must understand that there is a drought ahead. It doesn't matter which path you take. The important thing is to be on the path, because in that process you are ultimately trying to open doors. It's the process of opening doors that opens your life to the experience of that other plane. You're opening yourself to other possibilities. Now if you close that door, you never see what's going on beyond.

The important thing is that any spiritual path opens the door and makes you able to access whatever is to come. But you have to be in that process of opening doors. Trials make us stronger.

In terms of understanding our compassion in our lives, this life is not meant necessarily to be easy, because if it were easy, there would be nothing to grow from.

I'm not saying that you're going to suffer. You're not here to suffer; you're put here to enjoy. But it's the process of learning how to enjoy that's important—that you do not become a victim to an event, but derive joy from it, whatever the event may be. It can be a multitude of varied experiences. Some things that are seemingly negative in actuality possess germs of great enlightenment. There are changes coming that won't necessarily be comfortable for some, and I can't shield you from that. So it's an alarm that's being rung. A shift of consciousness, because, in essence, we have separated ourselves from the universe. And the universe is now drawing us back, is now saying, "Listen, you are a part of the greater whole."

You have to recognize that you can no longer deny that you are part of the entire cosmos. You do not function isolated. And somehow, in this plane at this time, we have gone off and become very disconnected from the rhythm that flows through all of us.

The rhythm is going to get louder. You're going to be forced to hear it. And those who shield their ears and close their eyes, yes, they will have to come back again to try to understand that process of being part of a greater rhythm.

The function of the ego is in many ways essential . . . and destructive. It's a paradox. It means to find a balance in the two. Our proclivity is to want to individualize to the point that we totally separate ourselves from All That Is, and in doing so, we are becoming destructive. There needs to be a balance.

So, with these events that we're talking about, these periods to come, there will be in some quarters a type of suffering. But that is part of the function of the whole process. I know it sounds contradictory, but there it is.

The truth of the matter is, there won't be trauma if you learn the lessons. You'll have an understanding of it. That's the whole quest.

It's all how it's interpreted, rather than being a victim to it.

The greatest lesson is that it is very individual. Again, it's not to say, "All right, everybody, stand by me now, and I will impart to you this kind of food for your soul." That's not what it's about.

It's about recognizing your connection. Your connection to the infinite, to All That Is. And remembering that, recognizing that. All the answers are already there. All the lessons you need to learn you've already learned on some plane or another. They're all part of this package. Because if you are part of the infinite, you are also part of the infinite wisdom. You have access to that. You now have all the answers you'll ever need.

It's creating access to it, refining that connection. And that begins by opening doors, by looking out and not looking to the side and being distracted. That becomes very individual. One person's way to open the door might be very, very different from somebody else's. There's no one way. And there's no one thing that I can say to you to avert what is to come.

For some people, it's essential that they experience what is to come. It's going to force them to deal with it—that's why it's appearing. There's a great discordance in terms of the energies in this plane now. They're fighting one another, trying to find their level. Trying to find their comfort. And in that process, in that upheaval, great change is coming.

Great change is coming. An ultimately wonderful change. It's like a whole renaissance, a rebirth. And in that rebirth, in that realignment of force, is a lot of pain.

When a woman gives birth to a child, it's a great deal of pain and then there's life. But it grows out of that trauma, the phoenix rising out of the ashes. It's part of the whole cycle of life and death.

Suffering is not necessarily something that needs to be avoided. It's incredibly beneficial if viewed in the proper perspective. And what we do is train ourselves through our spiritual paths to view this suffering in an enlightened viewpoint to see how it will make us expand our growth within the universe. Then it becomes essential; it becomes fulfilling. For the whole experience.

Some people will never hear it without trauma itself. Others will. And others will interpret it in a way that will propel them farther along their paths. I insist people get on the path. Get on the path, you know. When these events take place—these various kinds of occurrences—it will propel you. You will learn how to use it. But you've got to be on the path; otherwise you are aimless.

The pain of childbirth has a function. There is a function in terms of the force of the energy coming through. This energy field that enters and comes alive needs to have space made for it, in terms of its impact on the environment. And that process is like breaking the sound barrier. That force of energy is working against the elements to provide a new manifestation of this particular energy's form.

The most wonderful thing that happened is when Eve ate the apple. Had she not, Adam and Eve probably would have been profoundly bored. I'm speaking metaphorically here, of course—that life is not about lying about and having comfort. That is not why you come to Earth.

You come to recognize your value in the vast cosmos, in terms of your recognition of That Which Is in your life. It's sort of a game that's played. You come here with your memory erased of the profound connections you have. And then the game is who recognizes it first. Not that it's competitive—it's certainly not.

But do you recognize it in this life span? Do you reconnect and find the way to use that force in your environment to enlighten others around you, to increase the vibration of the quality of the experience? You give back to that. You find a way of connecting to that. Because you are separated. And then your goal, if I were to put it in such a way—your goal is to reconnect to it: separation, reconnection.

You need to understand the mortality. There is an experience that is to be had that is unique in this plane—the seemingly mortal coil that we experience, that there is a beginning and an end. We come to that with this information.

Sometimes—well, often—it is essential that this perspective be there so that the experience is fully realized. In other words, that you really take the time to smell the flowers, because time is limited. Well, in actuality, time is infinite. And there will be other sorts of metaphorical flowers to smell in the future.

But if you knew that coming in, there would be no attempt to really understand the plane you're in now, in terms of the value of the preciousness of the moment. If it was just that *I am going to be here for X amount of imagined time, and I'll just sort of sit this out until the next lifetime rolls around,* there would be nothing special about the experience.

Part of what is special about the experience is the illusion that it has a beginning and an end. And that sort of gives it structure in terms of the experience of it. The quality of every moment that comes along, of the preciousness of that individual moment.

Now, once you start that process, add to it later the knowledge that it's infinite . . . *infinite.* If it's an infinity in terms of the whole structure of the life force, it even further enhances that rose that is being smelled.

In other words—I'm trying to give you a very clear analogy of it with the rose—here's a rose. If you come in knowing that you're infinite and that life will go on forever, you may not really look at it as part of the experience. You will not fully be in this experience. You won't fully have those energies flow into you if you are still rooted in some other plane.

To take full advantage of the plane you're in, you have to be rooted in it. And part of the rooting in this process is that beginning and middle and end. So you see the rose, and you start to appreciate it. Once in the process, you reconnect to the greater force that is—All That Is—the rose in it becoming more enhanced because you've had the background. You've come through the trial of it and then have rediscovered your connection. It's a very beautiful process, ultimately.

It's sort of like you bloom at the same time the rose does. If you can time it in such a way that you come to full flower with the moment, there it is—you become one. And then there's a deeper understanding of the eternity of life.

I think we sent Einstein here to explain time. It's not linear; it's all happening at once, and we shift through various planes at the same moment. This thing called time—certainly, two-, three-, four-dimensional planes—is a yardstick of experience that is imposed upon the life-forms in terms of their ability to regenerate. But in actuality, that is extendable; that is, it's infinite how you measure infinity. I mean, how do you measure that? It's an abstract. It's birth and death that give this timeline. When you see the larger picture eventually, if you're on your path, then you release that fear of death. Death is time. Time by nature has death inherent in it. And we measure things because of that act of death. You remove that from the equation and suddenly there's no reason for it. It is bigger. It's bigger than that. It's more multidimensional than that.

It's a question of accessing . . . accessing that knowledge . . . accessing that understanding, that reconnection, getting reconnected.

The simplest thing I could tell people would be to take the time to experience their true nature. And that is by being in touch with nature. Because nature recognizes it. It already is there. It already has the big picture. By putting yourself in that nature, that energy gets transfused to you in a very deep level, if you allow it.

Now, it can be as simple as meditation. It can be as simple as looking at the sea and watching the waves come in, but take your mind out of the process—the mind, which sort of creates the perimeters in terms of your viewpoint, puts the end stops, puts the curtains around what you see.

By removing your conscious judgment of what you're seeing, and allowing the infinity of that process to enter into your soul, you start to heal—you start to reconnect to that greater connection, to that infinity of what you are. And you begin to access the answers that you need in this plane. Very simply at first, and then more specifically as time goes on.

To find that moment where you're totally at ease—whether you're a Buddhist and you chant, or you sit on a mountaintop and sing, or you go to the shore and feel the waves flow through your life—that's the beginning. Now, whatever is written in books or what I say is only to bring you back to those very simple things. That very simple access. All any path ultimately does is just clear the way for that energy to flow through you for that connection to be made. Eventually it has to be that you allow it; you open that door for it. Open the door and let it come in.

Having accomplished step one, there really doesn't need to be step two, because you have all the answers . . . all the infinity that you'll ever be able to handle. It's there for you.

If there were a step two, I would say it is helping others open their doors by being an example. By being in touch with All That Is, and having that really fully manifest in your life. Therefore, you will affect those in your surroundings, and they will be attracted to the energy that has come through you. They will be magnetized to you. And that step is to help others open their doors.

How do you enhance communication? It's about tuning your instrument. It's like pointing your antenna in the right direction. First recognizing you have an antenna. You have a feel for it. You have a way to access it. And then honing it to the point where you hear it more clearly so that you begin to understand that voice from within that is there for all. Some people can hear through angels. Some people can hear it through strange apparitions that come to them. Others, you know, have a sense of a dream state where it talks through them. It's about finding the antenna that works best for you.

Accessing prayer for many people is their way of seeking. The difficulty with prayer is that sometimes the monologue is so loud from this end, there's nothing to be heard. In other words, the prayer in actuality is an attempt to listen, yet many people have turned it into a monologue that goes out. What you need is to let the information come in. You don't walk through the door; you just open it and it comes in.

Communication with nature is different from communication with humans. There is a different quality to it. What is wonderful about a spirit or being in nature and allowing that to enter into you is that there's no static, usually. In nature, certainly not. There is not a kind of static that is created. It works directly from your soul to the soul of nature, and you bond. An understanding comes from that bond. With communication there is so much that becomes cerebral that gets in the way. And sometimes . . . sometimes that cerebral intercourse can jump-start an instinctual response to the environment so that you begin to listen to your instinct, so that you understand a concept. But concepts are only good if they can be utilized. In the abstract, they mean nothing.

To read something on paper and to nod your head in agreement is a wonderful little exercise. But unless it affects your life, what use is it?

If the cerebral endeavor somehow leads you back to your instinct, where you start trusting your instinct and fortifying that, then that discourse that happens between people is of use—is essential. It can be essential for some people. *Some* people. That's the only way their egos will allow them to understand it—if it comes from someone who's much more "important" than they are. I find the concept so hysterical.

It's like me saying that this hand is so much more important than that hand. We're all of the same substance, and yet some people need to recognize or to pretend that there is some sort of "importance quotient" that goes on. And some people can only understand something if they think someone more important or more knowledgeable than they can impart it to them, because then *they* can become more important so that they can impart it to somebody else. And that's really not the case.

But in some people, the only way that they can access the knowledge is through someone they believe knows more than they. And the truth of the matter is, we all know; we're all connected to the same great force.

✸ ◇ ✸

(27)

WHEREVER YOU ARE, THERE'S A HEALING THAT CAN TAKE PLACE

We feel you here now and want you to express your deepest desires. You have long been part of That Which Is, and you have fought your way to a place where influence is in your domain. You may now allow yourself the leisure to be at ease with who you are and settle into the space that you are holding. You are anxious about a lot, and you mustn't feel the need to strive and grow in an agenda that has nothing to do with your reality. You already set in motion all those entities that will come to support you. So now you must just allow this force field to come through you and know that you are at a place where this is possible. We don't want you to feel like you are burdened or feel that you have been under stressful circumstances. Sometimes you operate by sheer energy that is depleting you. You must take care of who you are so that you can be of service to the world.

There is also within you the ability to reach into yourself and deal with issues that are deeply a part of you. You may have been in avoidance often and not dealing with the things that really propel you to go forward. You have put them on the side and have allowed yourself to be consumed by this path. It's time for you to start healing yourself, healing the disablement of your inner life. This is *your* ability. You have this access. And there is a sense of avoidance in some of this that you must now conquer.

So now let's see how we can go about this. Your energy is finely tuned. You know what works and resonates for you; you have that ability to settle into that vibration, and you can do this at will. But you must now find a way to do this for yourself. You must take the time to heal yourself in terms of the space you're in. There is a field that you have yet to discover that will bring you a new introduction to another dimension in your work. It has unity in its design, and you will be a part of this new vibration, only if you settle into your true nature, into your true self. And then it will resonate deep inside you. This means you have to find time to be with *you*. You must find time to settle into your own life. This tendency to run away does not always work. If you want to be of service, a greater service, and be in this new dimension, now comes the work for yourself.

You have to make space. You have to make time for this. You have to be at peace within your life. The energy that you create interferes with this new dimension. As you learn to handle this other vibrational force, you will do this as well, but it's on a deeper level. And in order for that to happen, there has to be incredible peace within your life. Incredible surety. Confidence. Not the kind of confidence that is worked at, but that is a part of you, that belongs to you. That does not have to be worked at or driven or shown. And that comes in silence. Comes in silent moments. I wish that you could hear a greater vibration, but it is coming soon. You don't think that you have all the abilities that you have, and you have much greater. There's more to come. But you have to do the work on yourself. This is where the space is. Create the space. Create the space.

You have a great deal to offer here. Concentrate on your own force, your own life force. Keep that in harmony. At times it's disharmonious otherwise. It is like a song. It is like hearing a melody that has your name in it. It has a vibrational quality that is completely your own, distinctly your own. And you're closing in on it, this total harmony with the universe. But you have one last step to go. And it'll create a breakthrough for you. You only need to find peace within your life.

What we want is clarity, not confusion. Work to clarity. Work to go to clarity. And that comes. That does come. But you must, must, must find space for *you.* Don't create an agenda where there's no space for you. For your life.

I'm sure you've experienced a rapturous joy that permeates your life at times. That is accessible to you at all times. And in order for that to resonate, you need to quiet everything else. *All* the static, *all* the force that drives you away, *all* the panic has to leave. You will find this. But you can't harm yourself in the process. You may be very driven, but now it's time to enjoy the ride.

The new level that's coming through is deeper and more profound. It has stature to it. It has dimension. It is profound. And there will be no mistaking it. It is what *is.* It's the very core of existence. When you tap into this, once you get it, there will be no mistaking it. *No* mistaking it.

How much do you want to drive yourself, and how much do you want your life to let you go where it needs to go (the second being the optimal choice)?

Sometimes an instrument is just slightly off-key, and at times doesn't create the vibrational pattern that it needs to, to be optimally effective. It's fine-tuning. Very much fine-tuning. You have to allow yourself to be sensitive, really sensitive, to that fine-tuning that will come through, that you feel. *You* feel. And it makes all the difference.

It's the same as if you were trying to call somebody, and you were one digit off. You're not going to find that person. But with only a one-digit alteration, you're now connected. And you're that close. You're in the neighborhood. Look, the way to find that digit is to create the quiet inside you, the peace inside you, the assuredness inside you.

What you need to do is simplify, however you can do that. However you can simplify. It has its own sort of rhythm to it; it has no discordant sound. There is the mundane, but the mundane impacts the energy. It's all the same. Healing is healing. I think you have to feel yourself become a little more malleable. A little less rigid about it. A little less intense. A little more accessible. Wherever you are, there's a healing that can take place.

(28)

THE ENTITY ITSELF KNOWS WHAT IT NEEDS

You are at the area of your existence where you are coming to a greater depth of range of energy. Your character is now changing in the way it needs to in order to release a different form of energy.

You have now graduated to a higher plane that will encompass different forces. You will expand your realm of influence by accessing these greater forms of energy. They are pools that you need to tap into, and you allow that force to surface in its own existence. Your life must allow this force to come through in a stronger method. You feel at times "at sea" when it comes to channeling the very specific energy with the people you come in contact with. It isn't a consistent flow.

This force is stronger than your resistance to it. What happens in your periods of working is that there is a resistance that surfaces, and this will overcome that resistance, this greater force that is coming to you. You have glimpsed it in the past, and it seemed to be ephemeral. It is coming to you in a stronger way, and you will experience it very shortly. Being able to process it through you will allow you to fulfill a greater need than you had prior.

It is part of your mission to understand that it is a process and that it will heighten its frequency as you allow yourself to feel the flow as you push other forces away. You're clearing a path for it.

There are obstacles that come in the viewing of this form, and you must separate them away like you would wheat in a field. You must create the path. It already is there; it just needs to flow. Right now it is not directed. It flows in various forms. And what you need to do is more laserlike. Allow yourself to create a clearer path for it to flow.

You need to understand that your significance, or your power, is not that in which it is playing currently. It is coming through in a different way. You have now understood much of what you are try-ing to accomplish. You have direct goals that you are trying to fulfill, and you will accomplish these goals as time comes into play. They are already predetermined. It's like you're playing a round of golf: There is around the dogleg a vision that will be fulfilled. You needn't worry about it or work so severely toward it. It will come of its own volition.

You need to spend your time clearing the path, clearing the path for your greater energy to come through; and it will, if you are just consciously aware of That Which Is, as it is being fulfilled. And you must feel this with your life. You must understand the significance in your realm. It is cranking up the volume of this vibrational pattern. It's like wavelengths that shatter glass. Prior to it, the glass just tremors, and it crosses a threshold and the glass explodes. Same way with this energy force: you're very close to turning it to the point where it will magnify a hundredfold. It is very powerful, and you must now just clear the path. It will be much more consistent, and you're on the verge of that. You just need to trust and allow yourself to quiet that energy around you . . . allow it to be at ease. It's now in a realm of tension. There's a tension attached. You must remove the tension. As you are channeling this, there is performance anxiety at times, and you need to release that.

Take that tension away from it, because it thwarts the flow. . . . It thwarts the flow. Don't enter into a healing with the viewpoint *I've got to perform.* Allow it to recognize its own vibrational pattern. And feel free to step back and allow it to do the work it needs to do without the anxiety attached. That diffuses the energy. It puts up a wall that deflects it and makes it more difficult for it to happen.

You must trust. Trust on a deep level the ease in which it can be accomplished. It has in the past, and will continue to grow as you see fit to allow it. But it's in your ballpark. You need to prepare yourself to access a greater realm and just recognize that it's a fact already accomplished. It's already a done deal, as it were. You needn't fear it or fear the lack of it or fear it disappearing.

You have to trust on a very deep level that your life is accomplishing the mission. And as you allow that trust to build, this force will come through in deafening ways.

In this process of healing, there are polarities that you fluctuate in: the vibrational pattern has peaks and valleys; there are extremes. The polarities are such that at times you're feeling this incredibly intense heat, and then there are times when you feel the chill of the focus of some sort of energy. It is not qualitatively different. Those forces, those separate polarities, like the cold, are different energy fields as they come into play.

Now, one isn't preferable to the other. It isn't that you always have to assume that somehow you have an attachment to the idea that a heat force is healing. There are times when this other energy, this other field, has a lot to do with the nature of the person you're healing.

You need to trust your instinct. Do not judge it. Do not question or second-guess it. Because when you are in that process of healing, and suddenly you feel cold, you start questioning the cold, and immediately you've pulled yourself out of the process.

It's the same way with heat. If you stand back and start to analyze *What is the process of it?* and *What is it I'm feeling?* and all the other minutiae that come with this process, you're not fully invested in the process itself. You must totally remove those kinds of thoughts as they are happening. The nature of it plays what is needed with the field that you're dealing with.

The people who come to you have their own field of energy. It needs to find its own rhythm, and perhaps some of the rhythms resonate with a colder feeling in terms of the vibrational patterns happening. Other times those vibrational patterns will allow heat to be released as a by-product.

There is, in the nature of the interchange of their field of energy and your field of energy, something very much like two chemicals being mixed. It is the result of those fields interacting. What happens is, sometimes it releases cold, and sometimes it releases heat. But it's in the nature of that interaction, that energy interaction, and they can change as it continues. It is never in stasis. It's always in process. It's always movement, and it is a flow. So it will change, but the important thing is not to judge it as it is happening, not to feel that it is something that needs to be changed. You need to remove your mind from the process of it when you're in it.

After your sessions, it would be nice if you would notate your client's experience and your own, perhaps, for your records; and perhaps later on you'll be able to put it together. But for the most part, in the main, it really is interactions with the fields of energy and what this produces. Sometimes there are barriers that need to be broken down. And sometimes the barriers that are hardest are those that are coldest.

The thing is to quiet your mind in the process as much as you possibly can. It's like a meditative state. And the closer you can get to that and just release the anxiety that's attached to the process of it, the clearer and purer it will flow, and it will resonate far more with your patient.

You must ask yourself what you are doing to accomplish any kind of quiet. Are you actively participating in something? If not, you need to. You need to find that time. It's crucial. I'm not saying this as something that's "Oh, by the way, if you have a few moments." It's something that is really integral to the process, and you will only be more successful if you manage that aspect of it. It doesn't mean that you have to take hours of meditation in the morning—that's not what I'm talking about. You have to find those moments in your life where energy can be supplied to you. And that can happen on a daily basis if you put yourself in that energy that is perfect and formed already.

Optimally, being in nature is where the energy is formed. It's not thwarted; it's not manipulated. It is what it is. It's pure in that aspect.

And because in nature there isn't any second-guessing in terms of the quality of it, it only releases itself. I encourage those who are looking for a deeper spiritual self to put themselves in nature, because the harmonics of it allow you, yourself, to hear the energy in a way you haven't heard it before and automatically realign your own energy because of its qualitative difference from what you bring to it.

The metaphor I'd like to use is: If you are singing off-key in a chorus—if you're singing off-key with *one* other person—it is very easy to continue to sing off-key. But if you put yourself into a chorus of a thousand or a hundred thousand, the sound becomes so deafening that you are forced to sing on-key. In that environment your energy automatically becomes tuned. It becomes connected. It becomes connected again.

The more time that you can find—15 minutes, 20 minutes—in your garden, where there are trees, where there is nature to be appreciated . . . the more you will derive energy from that nature. It will be like a tuning device. It tunes you and makes you more harmonious within your own system.

The more that you thwart that, the more that you escape from it . . . the more difficult it is for you to convey the kind of energy that you want to during your given day. Take the time to undertake this kind of endeavor, of being in nature.

Find the time; make the time. It will save you so much time on the other end—of needless worry, of needless energy being dissipated in strange ways.

The more that you can focus yourself early in the day, the better. The energy that you exude becomes more harmonious and is more accepted in your environment. It's absorbed more easily by those with whom you come in contact. It's purer. And day after day of not taking that time, it starts building up walls, until you get very thwarted such that you're forced to shut down. And we look at that as a reason to escape.

There really is a very deep need to reattach to something that's organic, that's natural. We sort of interpret it as being that our jobs are too much, and, you know, that there's too much chaos in our daily lives; and we look upon that as the reason we need to escape. But in actuality, it's much deeper than that. It's *because* we haven't attached that all that chaos exists. The entity itself knows what it needs. It knows what it needs to fulfill its desire.

You have been in touch with this process for some time: of allowing That Which Is to speak through you . . . that force to reconnect other energies to a greater energy. It is the process of connecting to the greater energy source. That's what comes through you into that person. It is their direct intravenous line from the lifeblood of the universe.

Often people who have come to you have become disconnected from any force in their lives. They've become victims to it. They're not empowered. Most of the people who come to you are not empowered. They're looking for someone else to give them that.

It isn't exactly the nature of the healing experience. It isn't that you're giving them that. It's that you're connecting them to the greater force that already rejuvenates them. They already have all the mechanisms to do that—they need to be jump-started. Some have been disconnected for so long that their lives have corroded and are cut off. And the contacts aren't even pure enough for them to be connected.

So what happens is that it's very difficult because of the walls of callousness that have grown around them—it's hard to connect through to them, because they are invested in being walled away and being disengaged. You, with your power, are trying to, again, connect them with whatever poor, small opening they have to this greater force, to this greater energy. Once they experience it, it can be self-generated. Once that is attached, that opening can become larger.

Once a person experiences their own healing, it can continue under their own self-generated circumstances. They don't need a facilitator—they don't need someone to remind them—if they choose to understand that they can heal their lives. Jesus said it long ago: you can "heal yourself" if you allow it. Now, these people who have come to you may be so closed off—are so isolated, are so not in touch with what that force is—that they need someone to remind them of the connection. And that is where you come in.

You connect them to that greater energy field that we're all a part of. That we're all made up of. And we're all one.

There are those for whom their direct mission is to open these doors. Eric has that mission. Fred's is that mission in a way. That opens doors for greater understanding. It is a facility that comes from life-times of experience.

There are people who are meant to do this work—who have vol-unteered for it, have specifically volunteered to come into this plane to help mankind. That is their mission.

There is a body of knowledge that gets collected, and sometimes people feel they can put on the robe of this type of process, but they may not have the fundamental understanding. Now, everyone can heal their own life. *Everyone* can. And oftentimes for these people who have experienced things with energy—the infusion of this energy that we were just talking about—this pathway suddenly gets cleared for them and starts opening, in a way.

It finds its own level, but initially it will have these surges. And sometimes the interference that they experience are these surges that are happening. So experiencing that doesn't necessarily mean they also have the ability to heal.

What is going to happen is that you will find that many are called, few are chosen. All you can do is open the door for them to expe-rience. All you can do is present the information—whether or not they're able to take it. Those people who really are meant to continue on with the work will automatically be motivated. It's like they're reminded, and a light goes on and that creates a greater desire, which creates more opportunity, which creates more success, which creates . . . do you see what I'm saying?

They will, in their own way, find their ability to manifest the kind of energy form that they need to commit in order to work, to continue. Those who don't have the track record, who don't have the wealth of experience that is necessary, *will*—but perhaps not in this lifetime, per-haps not in the next lifetime . . . perhaps in the lifetime down the road.

So you can't force anyone, or tell someone, "Oh well, you have a talent. You need to do this." They have to come to that themselves.

They have to feel it so passionately because it's a work of passion. Healing is about passion.

And you never need to fear losing the ability once you have it. It won't leave. It's something that only becomes greater. To lose it, you would have to eventually just shut your eyes to it. Purposely try to thwart it. Because once it appears, it only grows.

Now the other thing you really have to discuss with yourself is this: Those forces that try to thwart your work—those forces are your negativity being made manifest in them. The negativity that's in your life will manifest itself in an environmental way with other people. They will respond to what they feel in you. And those days when you feel sort of timid or tentative about your life or about your work, that will be reflected in those people saying, "Well, you know, you lose it." Because that is *your* life saying it. That is *your* doubt speaking.

When you hear negativity, it is a call for you to redirect your harmony. It's not to argue with them. It's not your quest here to say to them they're wrong. Don't waste your time trying to sway or disprove what they are saying. That is their *gestalt,* for want of a better word. It's like a red flag for the healer. What you need to do as soon as you see negativity or hear it or recognize it is say, "All right. All right. Now, I need to harmonize again. I need to regroup. I need to see this, because if I'm very pure on my energy, that red flag won't appear."

(29)

YOU MUST KNOW THAT
YOU ARE A MASTER

The master-disciple relationship has existed for all of time. The mentor and the student, the master and the disciple. It's the nature of relationship. You're being reminded of this. You came into this world as a master.

There are many master teachers in various areas of our environment. But you're being reminded that this is work that is important to your life. It really doesn't have anything to do with ego, because it's about serving. It's not about gaining. It's serving, being of service to someone . . . allowing them to have their life bettered because you're releasing your energy as you serve them.

In some societies, this whole idea of "master" is having throngs of people at one's feet. That's not the connotation here. What we're talking about is that you have come here with a certain level of ability to serve, and you have volunteered to do that. You have made it your mission to come into this space to serve humanity, to bring up the vibrational level. And this is to remind you that this is your mission. You already know it.

So when you hear that, the benefit of knowing that is to be reminded of the kind of service that you can manifest. That you can generate. The kind of impact that your life in this plane can have on many, many people, without feeling "apart from." It isn't them and us. It's us and us.

The more you separate, the less successful you are. The more you're at one with the person in the room, the more you allow yourself to serve . . . the more successful you will become. It's not about ego. It's about accepting. Accepting your role.

There may on occasion be those who question the monetary value of your work. That is manifest negativity, in a way. That is *their* negativity. And what they're saying is that somehow they're not allowing themselves to be part of the process, you know, because they have this financial concern about it. *I should be able to get this for free because it is part of nature and I am a part of nature, and it should just be a process that happens.*

Money concerns are not easily measurable from person to person. Everyone has their attachments to it—the concern, the financial concern. Many people have a lot of esteem issues dealing with money—a *lot* of esteem issues—because it has become a measurement of validity in this society, unjustly so. And we have bought into the concept of our worth being measured in a monetary way.

So a lot of times those people who think you are "charging" for it are finding that there is some sort of egocentric thing, perhaps, that's happening with you that you are thinking that you need to make massive amounts of money because of your special skill. That's more their projection than anything to do with reality. That is just their negativity being generated.

And you needn't concern yourself with them. They have to come to terms with that themselves. What you can purely say is, "This is part of our bargain. This is our exchange. Now, you can make this exchange if you choose to, or you cannot. It's your choice. It is not my choice to change your viewpoint about it. It's not part of my role to justify or not justify this financial concern."

Finance is meant to help people be in contact with a greater self. We're not talking about immense wealth, but food has to be put on the table. That's essential, you know. And you mustn't feel timid about saying this is part of the nature of exchange.

Everyone is given gifts. Let's start there. Many gifts are rewarded. The gift to play a concert piano—that person is given a gift. Now, do they benefit from it financially? Yes, they do. Because they've worked very hard at their craft, and they know how to communicate with it. And the better they are at doing that, the more they get paid.

Sometimes people can only understand if there is an exchange, if it is of "value." It isn't always in the recipient of the financial exchange. It is also in the person, you know, who is the patient reaching out. Sometimes they have to develop their life. They have to make a sacrifice, seemingly—which it isn't—to empower their own life. Sometimes they will only understand it if there is a price tag.

For instance, let's say the bum on the street corner had the cure for cancer, had the *real* cure. No one would utilize it, because it's packaged wrong. And he could very well have the cure. Sometimes a person has to see the packaging before they can buy into the concept. That's just human nature. So sometimes it requires an exchange in order for them to accept that it's legitimate. The challenge for them is to come up with the money because their life is important and deserves that, and it honors their life.

The question is "fair"—what is fair? And that's something everyone has to determine in their hearts. What's fair for one group of people is not necessarily fair for another group. What *is* fair? If it's a million dollars for a healing, maybe that's not fair for everyone—the extreme. If it's free, maybe it's not right for every person. That's the extreme. So somewhere in the middle of all of that, "fair" exists. And that is something that you really have to determine in your heart. I think you are able to find that. You *are* able to find that.

And sometimes the recipient needs that challenge—needs that challenge to honor the exchange. That's a part of their gestalt. They need to make the sacrifice so they can take that into their lives. It's not really a sacrifice, but seemingly to them at the time it is. Because it's about their growth. Sometimes people won't honor it unless there's a price tag.

It's the intention of the recipient. Sometimes you might do something for free simply because the person, the recipient, is so earnest in their desire to change their life. You can feel it when you meet them.

There's a lot of gray in this world. We want to think in terms of black and white. Just as there are many, many human beings, there are that many different kinds of relationships.

The world is based on one-size-fits-all, and that's what people respond to; sometimes those lines need to be drawn. But there should be flexibility. And you'll feel it. Establish what your value is and what you're communicating, for the recipient as well as the person who is the healer.

Justifying the financial arrangement is unnecessary. It's totally unnecessary. All you can do is present the facts. Whether or not, again, people choose to participate is their choice. Oftentimes that is their negativity being reflected in terms of their attitude toward their healing. And toward their ability to allow themselves to be healed.

They're looking for some way to stay in stasis. To stay somewhere in un-health. And if they can attach it to the financial concern that helps them stay in the spot where they need to be, then they will attach that. So it will go: "Well, you know, I really can't be healed because you're expensive, or you charge an amount of money for my health."

That is them saying, *I really choose not to be healed. I am comfortable with my dis-ease. I don't want to break through that.*

If you approach it perhaps from that viewpoint, not attacking or finger-pointing on any level, but in terms of their desire—what is their *desire* for health?—and if they don't want to participate in that, then there's part of them that still wants to be unhealthy.

And sometimes that will surface when you, the healer, are weakest. *You* then need to retune. You need to retune your life. Tune it up. Find those moments. I can't overemphasize the need to do that for your life, because when you're not in tune or not in harmony, decisions are made that are not in your best interest, because you're making them out of vulnerability as opposed to strength. Your decisions are then being made out of need but not out of vision.

When you heal, it is a reconnection. A reconnecting. It's about reawakening their own innate ability—jump-starting them to experience it. It just so happens that you clear the path for that. You're connecting them with their higher energy form. And you're allowing them to experience that. It's like you're allowing the blood to get through.

In the same way, we have those paths of energy that we come to, into this plane, with which we are very connected. And due to the experiences of our lives, we start shutting them down—due to trauma, due to a lot of other things. It is our goal as healers—as you are a healer—to remind those people and let them experience, again, that connection. And eventually it can self-generate. They can regenerate their connection to the force. But it is the nature of energy and the vibrational patterns that resonate with the life. You're like a tuning fork in a way: you ring this true sense of energy, and the body comes up to it and accepts it and comes into some sort of vibrational pattern where the energy can be accepted. It's not discordant. It's not breaking down as it hits the energy field. It's accepted.

You must think of yourself—rather than as a healer—as a *facilitator.* Someone who facilitates the transfer of energy. The healing, if you will, is an agreement. And it's on a vibrational level. It's the person who's wanting to be healed opening their life up to accept that energy from which we all came and have become disconnected.

It's reawakening that connection and allowing ourselves to be connected with That Which Is. That is what we all are. Manifest in various planes of existences. But at the core of it all, we're connected, one to another. And I think part of what has happened in this world that has created so much discordance is that we are not aware that we are all connected. That battling one another isn't of benefit to anyone.

If we truly understand that the person we hurt is really part of ourselves, we'll go a long way into creating world peace. Right now we don't recognize that. We don't understand that we are all one essentially. We spend a great deal of time talking about how individual we are. And how special our nation, our race, our personage is, instead of expending any kind of energy to discuss how much we have in common.

We want to be apart. We don't want to be *a part of.* I'm going to leave you with that thought.

(30)

WE CREATE EVERY SECOND OF OUR LIVES— IT'S OUR ARTWORK

I am here for you now. We have been waiting for some time to communicate our energy with you. We feel your need for contact. We have wanted to let you be a part of that which has come to you before. There is in your life a need to express a new, divine type of communication that you have thought you had experienced.

We now know there is a different form of energy that is coming at this moment. You need to realize your facility with this newer kind of energy. It will help you to understand an avenue of existence that before has been closed to you.

We know that you have this kind of capacity for this expression. You haven't explored this territory yet, but you will feel it as it starts surfacing in your life. We know that this is of paramount importance to a further realm of success. Now is the time when you need to embody this in your life. It is not outside of you.

So you need to find a way to access this through your life without judgment, without interpretation of your existence. This will come to you organically as you move into this next realm. There is much that you have tried to do in the past, and you have felt thwarted in many areas of your life. You need to acknowledge these kinds of barricades and allow them to dissolve in front of you. Running into the barricade will not further your plan. You must allow them to find their space in existence and then dismiss that, without putting energy to it.

As we continue onward in this quest of yours, you need to center yourself in a different way than you have previously. You must ground yourself in a different kind of base, where the strength comes in through the bottom of your life. It comes through you and out. You need to give yourself the time to develop this. If there has been conflict in your life, you need to create space around it. You need more space.

You really are in control of that, but it has to start with your inner peace first. It can't be addressed to the environment. It has to have your foundation in there first. You must embody that kind of peace. And then it will communicate. You can't fix the shadow. You have to stand up, and the shadow will stand up.

Inner peace is a rhythm of life. It is a connection with the universal energy, the cycle of it. It is getting in rhythm with the music of the universe. If you're fighting the music, the sound is not very delicious. You must find a way to harmonize with the universe, and that comes from being at one with yourself . . . *being*. Taking the time to prepare yourself before you interact with the people around you. You must feel that rhythm in your life, and you'll know it as soon as you feel it. Too often you forge ahead without establishing that kind of foundation first, and the result is that the music becomes dissonant, and it hurts people's ears when they hear the communication.

You must find a way to be at one with yourself and at peace. That may take some time before you proceed, but you need to *take* the time. You're very much at the effect end of things now. You have to be at the causal end. And that's easily accomplished with a simple adjustment of your consciousness. But you need to take your time with it.

You need to create space for it. That means you *have* to create space for it. It means that you have to allow time to be at one with yourself, scheduling in the time. You can't run from communication to communication.

There are many ways of going about it, but you really need to take the time to just sit with yourself quietly, removing all of that negative kind of static that comes into your life. That has to be turned down. That volume needs to be turned down. And there's a lot of static going on, and it's stopping you from becoming really power-ful. It's thwarting you. You must eliminate the static. The message is harder to receive when there's static.

There is energy that can be accessed by everyone. Everyone in this world has a conduit to this, as you well know—this kind of energy. Now, what you need to do is define the conduit and find the way that best can be connected to the larger energy.

Once people feel the peace of That Which Is within their lives and their connection, it's much easier to proceed in their daily existence. That realm that can be accessed is something that perhaps you might want to investigate. How do you as a spiritual being connect with the larger being?

That will allow people to find their way to the realization that they are one *of* many; not one *from* many. The greater consciousness that we all feed into. And there's communication on that level, on the "greater consciousness" level, that can be accessed. What hap-pens often is we divide—we restrain ourselves. We build walls around us. We hide ourselves from these energies because we're afraid of the power that we have. We're afraid that we will truly be powerful in our lives. We look to others to strengthen us, which is a no-win proposition.

Fears come from the fear of the responsibility of life—that once you are responsible for your life, that's the key. People don't want to have that responsibility. They want to be in a state of need. They want "need" in their lives. Somehow that becomes the generator for their existence, where in actuality, need is an obstruction. Need is what keeps us from connecting. If we all knew that we didn't need these things in our environment, and we have all the power we want if we connect to the larger consciousness, what would we do with our tim

Trying to protect yourself with crystals and amulets is fear based. It is fear, based on negative energy, instead of allowing yourself to recognize it's an illusion. It's this need to be dependent that attracts you to these other objects instead of taking your own power in.

It's, again, not owning your power. *If I get the right crystal, then I'll be powerful.* It's looking for completion outside of yourself instead of recognizing that the completion already exists. We're looking to complete ourselves from the outside. *If I have this amulet, if I have this crystal, then I'll be powerful.* Well, in that case, the power is fully outside of you.

You're endowing those objects with power or protection or whatever, and you have no control over your life because the amulet has the control. The crystal has the control.

We're passing our power away. People are afraid of taking real responsibility for their lives. And we've been trained in this society to look to others. Some religious dogma requires having someone intervene for us because we cannot do it on our own. And that's misguided.

The practitioner has to remove the ego from the healing approach when they feel like they want to add something to make themselves "more" or wear the costume or the special clothing, or move clockwise instead of counterclockwise as well. You know, it is a channel that everyone has access to. *Everyone.* Everyone has access. It's clearing the way. You know, being able to see that connection with the larger consciousness, because there's every obstruction in the world to *not* let us see it.

Sometimes people want to medically intuit—somehow diagnose through a pendulum or guides—to find the problem. To diagnose it and then try to fix it according to what we understand, instead of being willing to simply become the observer and be present as a catalyst for the healing.

This is a really large topic to address. One of the reasons we're introduced to life on this plane is to make that journey from powerlessness to power. We come in coded with the fact that we're reliant on someone else; and in essence we *are,* on our parents, you know, s we are children.

That encoding happens almost organically, and we believe that that is the way we must proceed for all of our lives, because we have transferred all of our power to our parents initially, but then there comes an awakening. There is a journey that happens, and eventually we become ourselves. We become our own parents. We reclaim that role for ourselves. And when we parent ourselves, we become self-sufficient. We become the whole being that we can be. And that's a hard concept for many people to grasp, how we parent ourselves and shift it. So that's one of the journeys that happens—this transition from a dependent to an independent, self-reliant individual.

But too often that level of consciousness never gets broken. We then pass it on to a mate. We pass it on to a friend. We create that type of "you need to be there for me" codependent relationship. All of those kinds of paradigms that exist in society. And somehow the journey is to reach the point where you become full, in and of yourself, accessing the energy that exists for everyone. It isn't a limited pool. It's unending. One only need reach. And sometimes it takes a little effort. But that's where the harmony comes in—when you're able to reach and feel that fully in your life, that center where you are not reliant, where you own your life.

So many people don't own their lives. They've sold parts of it, given it to people. And then they try to reclaim it and get frustrated because that person, they say, took a part of their lives, as opposed to that they *let* them take part of their lives.

It's about reclaiming your life after your early years as a child. It is making yourself whole again. It's so easy, when it seems that all you have done is *given,* to get into the drama of life. It all becomes a drama, where we now have people to blame for our deficiencies because they did something to us or we perceive they've done something to us. And now we're victims, and we can be very comfortable in our victimhood and look for someone to save us from that. Yet that will never lead to a fulfilling life, because the power is not them. It is here. It's here, here *inside* you. You don't need to pull from other people and have that fight, that war.

It's remembering. It's a process of remembering, because when we are not in this plane, we recognize it. We understand that connection and we give it up only in order to find in this life the journey to rediscover it again, and change our environment by doing so. So a part of the mission of every human being born in this particular plane is to reclaim their power—to remember their power that they have let go of before they've come on this plane.

It is very much like a treasure hunt. We've all come on this plane to participate in a treasure hunt, and the treasure is within us. And until we recognize it, we're always going to be looking for treasure outside of ourselves. There comes a moment that turns into the "Aha" moment. We actually realize that the treasure is who we are, and we respect that for what it is. We all are treasure.

That's the rediscovery. We are all here to play this game.

If you are at one with yourself—if you are really in tune with your inner life—no choice you make is wrong. There is value in every choice you make. It doesn't matter. It doesn't matter what choice you make. Some people think, *Should I go through this door, or should I go through that door?* And they spend a whole lot of time trying to decide which door to go through. They all lead to the same road. But we're stuck trying to find a way: *Which door should I choose? Does this door have value, or does that door have value? Is there treasure behind this door, or is it behind that door? I don't know. Maybe I need someone to help me figure out which door it is.* And they spend this time in this sort of purgatory-life existence where there's no movement.

The thing is to pick a door and walk through it. It's going to take you where you need to go. You don't have to worry about making the wrong choice. Because there's value in every moment; there's value in every choice—there's a lesson in every choice you make, should you choose to see that. It doesn't matter. Move. Go through the door. Don't contemplate the doors. *That one is prettier. That one looks pretty severe.* It doesn't matter. It doesn't matter. Go through the door.

If there is any choice that would be the least desirable or closest to wrong, it would be to not make a choice at all. And some people back off. *I'm not going to go through any door. I'm comfortable here contemplating doors. That's where my existence lives. I'll watch other people walk through. I don't know what's happening on the other side of it, but 'll let them choose. I'll wait to see how many go through this door, and*

I'll wait to see how many people go through that door. I'll get opinions on the doors. I'll have them measured.

So all of that fear is about deciding, which doesn't matter. It doesn't matter. Move. People don't move in their lives. They don't grow. They become very accustomed to the room they find themselves in, and that can be very painful sometimes. We all know those people who are invested in their pain. In those cases, they need to move. It doesn't matter which direction, which way. It doesn't matter. But where they are is where the pain is, and the growth is in the movement. The insight is in the movement, not in the stasis.

It's about getting people to move—move in their lives. Spiritually move.

People may not always demonstrate the healing that you believe they should be receiving. Your role is to realize you have an ability to connect them to a higher energy. Sometimes people's maladies—their deformity, their lack of energy in any part of the body—are all part of something they need to experience to learn the lesson they need to learn. Sometimes they refuse to learn the lesson of what that condition brings them. And sometimes they need to stay there until they learn the lesson, whatever it is, from the limitation—from whatever. If it means deepening in compassion for something, then they can release it.

None of this is accidental. None of these maladies that come in are accidental. They are there for a purpose. They serve a purpose. And until people understand the purpose of that, the lesson hasn't been learned.

As a healer, all you can do is present an opportunity, and sometimes a very good opportunity. That's all you can do. There can be no attachment to the outcome. Again, it's providing a door. There is a door that is opened. Do you choose to walk through it or not? We open doors. As healers we open doors to energy. We open doors to a larger, fuller existence.

We open doors to a life that is in harmony with the universe. We open doors. Now, whether or not that person is able or willing to walk through that door is their gestalt, is their challenge, is the reason they were born into this plane. No one was given these maladies by accident. There's a bigger lesson to be learned.

Let me be very clear here. It's not a lesson that needs to be learned cerebrally. Sometimes it can be on a cellular level. And they are willing to accept and appreciate the malady for the compassion it gives them, the insight that they never had. Unless they can find a way to start looking at these things as opportunities to change something deep in their lives—to deepen their lives—they are not going to heal. This is their opportunity for growth.

Every malady we have, every obstruction we have, is an opportunity for us to grow. They are unique experiences. They're all various experiences that shine a light on a different part of That Which Is. For some lifetimes we view it from this viewpoint, and it becomes very closed and myopic. And other times, we give ourselves the opportunity to be more expansive in our viewing of the nature of that sculpture from another angle. And sometimes we have to walk around the entire sculpture to understand its true beauty and nature. As healers, all you can do is point that out and say, "Here is the door. Are you ready?"

So, the more varied the experience that we give ourselves, the better our understanding of this whole experience . . . this whole plane that we're being a part of.

And whether we make our choices on this plane from fear or love—it doesn't matter, because there is a gift to be gained. It doesn't matter.

Choices are choices. The value you put on them is a construct that is foreign to the universe. You're putting values on these choices— fear, love, or whatever. You know, you're qualifying the choice. The choice is the choice. It's to take you where you need to go. It doesn't matter if it's fear or love based, or however you want to qualify it. It is for you to move through it and to find fulfillment on the other side of it—the compassion on the other side of it.

If you start analyzing, *Is this fear based?*—now you're in stasis. You're looking at doors.

The same level of healing will not be brought through by the practitioner who cowers in fear and protects themselves in flames and tual as it would by that same person if they stepped into feeling a freedom of love and interaction with the universe. What needs to happen is that all of the judgment needs to be taken out of the equation.

All of that judgment, all of that. In other words, if you have a healer who has amulets, let's say, to use an example—or crystals—for protection or whatever, they are not really embodying their power. They have a journey to make. If they are utilizing something outside of themselves, they are reliant on some other power. So, in essence, they have not fully empowered themselves, and they *lack*. The energy *is*. It *is*. End of story.

Now, are you going to obstruct it with crystals and amulets and ritual and . . . ? Is that what you're going to do, obstruct the clear flow? It's like decorating a hose. *Maybe I'll tie this around it; maybe I'll tie that around it*—and then the water doesn't flow.

There is not one thing you can do to help "open" yourself up to fully interact with your sense of sight or sound. It's not the job of the hose to recognize the water. Part of it is your nonjudgment of the process—your removal of judgment, your neutrality about it—that makes it successful. If you were to hear this, if you were to interact, you would no longer be serving a purpose.

It's the energy of the person . . . that's what's going on. You are the conduit to allow that to happen. If you, as a conduit, start stepping back and *not* serving that function anymore in a purely neutral, nonjudgmental manner, then the whole connection breaks down because now you're stepping out beyond it. You're not in there anymore to allow that to happen, that force. Your role is purely to be a conduit. It's an important role. Make no mistake about it. Make no mistake about it.

Many people feel, for example, that crystals will help. It's a function of ego. Because they believe that they have the answer. "*I* have the answer. Come to *me*. *I* have the answer. That person over there doesn't have the answer. *I* have the answer." It's all a function of ego. "That separates *me* from him. *I* have the bigger crystal; *I* have the bigger amulet; *I* have the words to speak that he [or she] doesn't. Now, you have to come to *me*."

Again, we're assuming that there is a limited source of power, that *I have more power; they have less power.* And it separates us from the healing process. The more that we can strip away all of that and just be very present . . . what comes back to you, what you create, is the time—the creation of time to be very present in your life. So many people have talked about this in so many different ways, and still it is never heard. You really need to be present in your existence without functioning out of ego and just feeling the power that is.

People are running around everywhere looking for power, and they already have it. They spend their whole lives scurrying from shop to kiosk trying to find the one who has the power. All they have to do is stand and look in the mirror and they'll recognize: *This is truth. This is truth. It's already here. It's here in this second, in this moment.*

And people are in the business of giving it away. We've got to reclaim it now. We have to recognize that we can be fully animated in our lives and not at the expense of anybody else. That we can be fully happy and present in our lives and not at the expense of somebody else. And for some reason everyone thinks there's only "this much" resource in the world, in the universe; and there's only this much happiness to go around. *If that person takes too much happiness, will that leave so much less for me?* No. It's unending. Totally unending. It's limitless.

We were born to celebrate our existence, and too often all we do is mourn. It's a crime, but that's the journey. That is the journey from going from mourning to celebrating.

Whether we try to figure out if we should walk through the mourning door or try to figure out which is the celebration door, there's still growth yet to be had. Just walk. Walk; move. Because in movement, the revelations come. When we simply stand, nothing gets revitalized; there's no recognition. That's when we get stasis. It's all cerebral. We don't trust our instinct. We don't trust our lives, the sum total of experience. We don't connect to that vast pool of energy that exists.

Let's say you had to dig a hole through the earth to the other side, and somehow you say, *I'm going to do it without a shovel. I'm going to come in and do it without automatic bores. I'm just going to do it with my arms, my hands.* Well, you can do it, I suppose, but why would you? Why not get yourself a shovel? And that's the power that's in your life. That's the journey.

We spend so much time looking for other people's shovels. *You got one? Great.* Instead of claiming our own power. Using our own shovel.

Responsibility is a very loaded concept. It's as if you created something to deserve this, and you're being punished for past lives, and this is your punishment. And that's not very creative. It only further reinforces victimhood.

I think the way you need to look at it is that these are opportunities, as dark as they may be, to examine your life in a different light. What positive energy can you derive from that experience? Within every crisis, within every confrontation we have in our lives, within every obstacle we encounter, there is growth manifested at the same time. And I think that people need to be very creative in terms of being able to take that crisis, that obstacle—whatever you want to call it—and then turn that into *Where is the growth from the experience?* Is it to make you more compassionate, work for better laws? Do you see what I'm saying? Or is it for you to better understand the side of yourself that you didn't understand before? Or is it to widen your compassion for humankind? Whatever. There is in that moment, in that crisis, growth to be mined. So it becomes much more creative than: *I'm taking responsibility. What did I do to deserve this?*

What did you sign up for when you came into this lifetime? What were the challenges you set up for yourself? It isn't that you came to "experience" and just be. It's like you created a syllabus before you ever got here. Then, through your going through the syllabus, you have graduated into whatever level you want in terms of your growth. You laid out the obstacle course. You chose the circumstances in which you were born. You chose the things that you were going to have to confront. You made the hurdles higher. That's where the creation comes in. Before you ever were put into this plane. It's a challenge. Life is a challenge in the good sense. The challenge is for the participant to overcome these obstacles, and in the obstacles is growth. There's growth in every single obstacle you'll ever encounter.

So, in terms of responsibility, are you responsible? Yes, you are responsible, because you set up the obstacle course for yourself before you ever came here.

It's so easy to say to someone, "Take responsibility." It's like, *It was your fault. Now deal with it.* And that comes with a lot of negative baggage, and that's how people interpret responsibility oftentimes. They don't see it as the creative force that it can be. What we need to do is just alter that perception. I think the concept of *responsibility* is sometimes too loaded. I think what you have to do is say: All right, this is existing in your life now. How can you, through dealing with this experience, strengthen your life force? How can you change that?

In life we are creative. We create every second of our lives—it's our artwork. The color we put on the canvas is color that we've chosen to put on the canvas. But we selected the paint when we were on the other side.

What I'm saying is, your selection of the paint and how you paint with it is going to make a difference in terms of how vivid and alive the picture is or how dead and victim-like the picture is.

That's the creation you're creating. That's the picture you're creating. Are you picturing a life that is blooming and blossoming and growing? A life that faces no adversity is very un-colorful. There's no character. There's very little compassion. We see this time and again. The easy life is *not* the easy life. There's no dimension. It's only when you choose to challenge yourself on this planet that great work comes, great art comes. Great music comes from that creative energy. *Do I do this, or do I do that? Do I illuminate the condition, or do I hide the condition?*

So, if you choose to hide or internalize all of that, then the challenge gets harder because at some point it has to be transferred into something positive. At some point; otherwise you die from it. You become victim to it. It's about transforming. Transforming the energy that you have—the circumstances that you're having—and becoming more vivid in the living of it and more creative in the process of it.

Sometimes it takes a while. Sometimes it takes a couple of lifetimes, you know, before people understand that there is growth in those situations. There is a jewel embedded in every dusty rock. *How do I get to the jewel? How do I get to it? How do I illuminate it?* Too often you take the rock and you throw it away. The rock comes rolling back. You take the rock and you throw it away again. And again the rock comes rolling back. You take the rock and suddenly there's a little chip in it, and *then* you discover the potential inside. *Oh, wait a minute. Oh, oh, ohh!*

Sometimes the rock has to be thrown back at you a couple of times before you start to see what it is, the opportunity that it is. It's about strengthening your life force and transforming what seems to be a bit of coal into a diamond. But we often just dismiss it. *Oh, it's only coal. I don't want to deal with that.* And a missed opportunity happens.

That's where I think the shift in consciousness needs to be really examined—about finding the jewel in every experience that you have and every confrontation that you have, with every interaction that you have. It can put a positive spin on your life and become something of value, or you can use it to become a victim. There's no other choice. Every experience. *Do I go forward or do I go backward in terms of my human evolution? Do I go forward, or do I go backward? Do I deal with this now? No, I don't want to deal with this now.*

If you don't want to deal with it now, wait a while; you'll deal with it later. Because you set that course up for yourself. You wrote the syllabus. And it's a challenge. It is a challenge. But when you break through, that's where the essence of joy is. Joy comes through being able to handle a circumstance and create value out of it and move forward and let it propel you to higher levels.

For example, forgiveness is directly tied to compassion. To take an extreme example, if someone killed a member of your family, it's very hard to forgive the person who did that. It's very hard. However, if you can find a way to create that kind of depth of compassion for the rage and anger that exists in that person, *you* become a better person. You become fuller as a human being.

You understand nature that much more than anyone else. No one kills anyone because they decided they had nothing better to do on a Saturday night. There's a whole history of energy that comes with that act. And sometimes this is very hard for people to understand. Sometimes people come in with that mission. They are like a part of the play that you cast, and they serve a role so that you can grow.

People volunteer for different roles all the time. Volunteer for the four-year-old who's going to be hit by a truck. *I'll do this role this time for you. I will do that for you.* Now, can you find a way to transform that into a positive life force that can reaffirm life? Can you find it in yourself? That's the challenge you have set up. You have decided to do that. So you bring your cast of characters in, and you do the play.

There are many planes of existence, Earth being one of the many. We all operate on various planes of existence, and sometimes simultaneously. There is the here-and-now that we believe is the reality of our lives, but there are parallel life forces going on. It's multilayered. And at times another part of this very real existence is in another plane at the same time that you experience what you perceive as this reality. It's in all these planes as well that we visit past lives through the subconscious and bring up information that is integrated into this plane like a massive reference library, as it were. In your dream state you are consciously searching through the books. Taking one down, exploring, putting it back. But we forget most of it, because otherwise we wouldn't be able to function clearly in this life. Instinct is the imprint of those books in our lives. When you open that door, there's a vast amount of knowledge that is given to you, and at times, some of it is very specifically realized in this plane.

So, it's like this plane is a great museum that we walk through time and again with a different persona. And from that different persona, we understand a whole different aspect of compassion, and we become far more compassionate in our nature, which is ultimately That Which Is—manifest compassion.

Find a way to allow yourself to harmonize with the greater spirit that is identified as *you* on this plane. You must be able to have completion in your soul. There is great information to come for you. Do not be afraid of your existence. Integrate all that's around you, and when you are about to sleep, ask to have wonderful information imparted to you. It's a great experiment at first. You will become more successful as you continue to do it.

Now, there are planes of existence where this cycle doesn't repeat the way that you see it repeat on Earth. Earth happens to be a challenge. It's a tough school to enroll in. It's one of the hardest. There are places where life isn't this adversarial. But it's like enrolling in a training camp, Earth. Do you follow?

"What's the toughest training camp I can sign up for?"

"You might want to try Earth. They have a very good program. It's very creative."

We don't understand. We talked before about colors. We sometimes believe there are, you know, 14 colors in the box, let's say. There are thousands of colors, colors you've never seen. The box here is almost empty. You fool around with maybe 14, 18 colors. There are colors beyond your imagination. But that's hard for people to absorb. That is hard for people to understand without alienating their audience. You have to understand that you have to make these things accessible in the beginning. They'll trust. And understand that every life is a possibility for growth and deepening compassion. Every second that you have. And to view everything that comes into your life as a growth vehicle for compassion and deepening your understanding.

Most people's thought processes don't go to what happens 15 worlds later. They are very rooted in the now. And you can't overwhelm them with the 180,000 colors that exist. You can't. They can't absorb that.

So you have to go back to the accessibility of it. Forgiveness exists to develop compassion, and those who do it best are remembered the most because they stand out. Like Jesus, another volunteer.

Each time you come back with a deeper understanding, you are sooner able to help others do the same. Again, you're trying to change the vibration of this planet, ultimately. The challenge is to try to somehow change this warring nature that exists into something that's positive.

You've heard the concept of old souls. Every time you come back, you have a deeper and broader understanding. You have more ammunition. You have a deeper and broader understanding of the human condition, and you're able to affect more people. That's your role. They look to you for that. They don't know why, but they do. And that is your function in this plane: to bring people to the light, to have them see the understanding in *this* plane, not after they move on to another one. In *this* plane. *How can I bring people to the light?*

Which is what you're doing, which is what Eric and Fred are doing, which is what you're all involved in.

The "light" being perfect understanding and compassion.

There is going to be great change in the future. Will the glass be half-empty, or will it be half-full? Again, it will all be dependent upon those who perceive it. For some, they will view it as a cataclysm; for others it will be a reawakening. But there is change coming. That is why these spirits throughout the universe are appearing. It is to prepare the path for the change to come. It needn't be feared if you have the understanding of eternity.

In many areas it's already in the process. The groundwork is being laid, and it will be profound as we move forward. Certainly, there will not be a day when "the earth stood still." It is a process that will come to each individual. They will find that their belief systems either work for them or suddenly they don't work any longer. Those who cannot hear will be homeless. And those who want to seek will find new homes.

(31)

THERE WILL NEVER BE ENOUGH APPLAUSE

The function of healers of all stripes in this existence is the possibility of opening doors. It is opening doors, as well, for your *ability* to open the doors. For your ability to have compassion to open those doors.

You have to have compassion for the person who's deciding whether or not to walk through the door, so that they will come through. Hopefully they will. You want that result because you want people to feel better about their lives. You want them to function in a clearer way, but you can't get attached to the result of it, and you can't internalize the result of it because that's not in your control.

In other words, if somebody is holding on to whatever sort of disease and they are adamant about it, that's no reflection of your ability to open a door.

You've opened the door. You've invited them in. Now, perhaps they just don't want to walk through it. That's no reflection of you, and that's not something that you can quantify to a degree.

You can only open the door. It's their challenge to walk through it. So when they don't walk through it, it isn't because you didn't open the door nicely. You opened the door. "So, come on in. And if you don't want to . . . next time."

If it's someone very close to you, like a spouse or a mother or father, it's very difficult because there's an emotional attachment there, as well, you know; and sometimes that can cloud the process. If you're too close to the person, then it doesn't become a clean relationship.

It's loaded, fraught with experience. And sometimes they won't hear it from you, but somebody else can summon them. Because they have all kinds of preconceptions wrapped around the color of the information that you are bringing forth. But persistence is a great quality of compassion. Never giving up on anybody, ever. It may not happen today. There's tomorrow. It may not happen tomorrow. There's the day after that. "I will continue as long as I am thoroughly able to, because I have compassion for you." Eventually their resistance wears down. Eventually, because compassion is stronger energy. It's stronger than their resistance. But it has to come from compassion. It can't come from, "Why aren't you doing this?" because that becomes irritation, and they interpret that as another type of thing entirely. And now they are justified in their stance because you are hounding them, and they are irritated by it and "She just won't let me alone."

If the message is delivered with true compassion—and that's something as a healer you have to examine—if it comes from pure compassion, eventually it will be heard. It *will* be heard. But impatience is not part of healing.

What I'm saying is about overcoming the negativity of their energy. Positive energy is far stronger. And it's no match if it comes from love and compassion. There's nothing that can stop that.

There's nothing that can stop a true flow of energy. Love energy and compassionate energy is stronger than all of the negativity you could possibly summon up. But you have to examine that yourself as a healer. You have to examine: *Am I coming from that position? Am I coming from 'I have another two or three appointments coming up, and I want to get this one out of the way'?*—that's not compassion. It really has to do with: *Do I really want to reach into this person's life and help them achieve a kind of joy that they have not known before? Is that where I'm coming from?*

It is totally a part of every interaction you'll ever have. It's clearer in a healing relationship simply because you usually don't know much about the person beforehand. And they are coming to you with a certain sort of willingness or hope that something will change. So that dynamic is different.

It's much cloudier when you get into interpersonal relationships, because there are histories and there are motives and there are agendas. But if, as a person, you examine that, eventually it rights the ship. You get on an even keel, and people trust you the way they haven't trusted you before, if you have real compassion. If you have *real* compassion. And you *want* that in your life, and you've found a way to find that.

That's where it has to start. It has to start from the heart. And the more you care about others, the more joy you will experience. Genuinely care. Not with an agenda to it. Genuinely care for another existence, because we all are one. Helping someone else makes us happier. It's a direct result, a direct result.

If you're so focused on making other people happy that you suffer, then you're not in the right space. Then your approach is wrong, because there should be no suffering attached to it.

Again, if you're suffering, you may be talking about suffering from the neglect of your own life. But there's a deeper truth going on here, where if you're using the healing as an avoidance of dealing with your own life or you're looking for the healing to validate you as a person, that's not a pure, compassionate agenda. Because now you've attached your self-worth to how well you can turn this person's life around. It becomes about you. "Aren't I grand, the way I opened this door?"

You're just opening the door. You hope and you try and you pray that they'll walk through it. But it has nothing to do with you as a person. It has nothing to do with how good or bad you are or however you view that in your life, your own self—or how you measure your own self-worth. If you do it—if you heal from a totally compassionate viewpoint, where you really are concerned about that person's life in that moment—there's real joy to be derived from that, from that process. There's a *real* joy. And what happens is that you become more magnetic. People are drawn to you.

It's as if you were going to be a grand actor; if you go into it so that people can applaud, there's never going to be enough applause. There will never be enough applause.

Being a healer is a mission. It's a mission of being compassionate. There is a focus—you can't deny it—about being a healer. There is a focus. There is a tangible result, but you cannot play victim to that result.

You can't look upon yourself as "less" or "more" depending upon whether the person walks through the door or not. You can't. Again, all you can do is open the door.

You cannot go into healing for the reasons of not experiencing the love you feel you deserve; or of not being complete on some level, and you feel this will give you completion.

In that case, you are looking for the applause of being onstage, without giving the gift for which you receive the applause. You are putting the cart before the horse. The agenda is all confused. It takes a lot of effort to come from a very pure place. The result is that the light will shine. And you'll be able to bask in that light because it comes from a pure place. If you don't come from that place, no matter how much light shines on you, it will never be enough. It will never serve to satisfy, because it starts with inadequacy, feeling inadequate.

$$\textcircled{32}$$

EVERYBODY'S INDIVIDUAL EXISTENCE IS A SYMPHONY

L ights have vibrational patterns. And it's all about the vibrational patterns. The light you see that you become a part of is different from the light of the sun. It's a different level. It's a different plane.

Again, it's the function of these vibrational patterns in an individual human being, even on a cellular level, that allows it to become alive. Between the atoms there is sound, and the sound is in wavelengths, in light waves . . . it vibrates. And that's what gives our existence its function, and we are a part of that vibrational pattern. Everything is vibrational. Light waves, vibrational. What we need to do is to become very attuned to those vibrational patterns. Letting light in, for instance, is allowing ourselves to harmonize with the light, to harmonize with the sound of light. It's not separate. It's a part of us. It's what feeds us. It's what makes the signal stronger in our lives.

And the essence is we are vibrational patterns. We are light waves. That's what we are—that space between the atoms that vibrates. And that's what we attune ourselves to when we do any kind of meditative process or whatever we want to do. If you are in silence, you will hear the sound of light. We need to coordinate our energies with that vast, bigger energy because it all is in wavelengths. There's a hum to it, and there's a sound of light.

So when it's discordant, it becomes directly in opposition to what allows us to celebrate our lives.

And what happens is that when it's unorchestrated in various organs, it creates disease. Reorchestrate your life through that sound, through that wave, because everybody's individual existence is a symphony. We've just got to get everybody playing the same tune by recognizing that. It's an oversimplification—but it holds. It holds. We have to orchestrate our lives, orchestrate our bodies, so that we're heard in a gentle and harmonious way.

Light breaks down into various bands of vibration, and some people utilize various spectra for very specific reasons. That is *their* avenue into some healings. But light is light. It is energy. It is energy, plain and simple. And accessing that light—that energy—again, it goes back to orchestrating our lives.

Now, everyone tends to make this very complicated, you know, and they tend to want to dissect it. It is much simpler than all of that. It is much easier to access than all of that. I think what happens oftentimes is people get very possessive of the way that light gets accessed, the avenue. "This is the avenue to take, and I'm the one that can lead you." Do you see what I'm saying? Here we go again.

You know, it's about, again: "I have the answer and you don't, and therefore I have more power than you."

Often people are trying to control the healings by specifying colors instead of allowing the clear light to flow in, and allowing the intelligence of the universe to control it.

It's becoming about "the knowledge that I have that you don't." But, if you shine a clear white light on anything, it is going to fill in wherever there are gaps.

It's going to heal itself; it's going to find its level.

You know, it's going to find its level. But the choice of How do I direct the very specific kind of light? is, again, a thing of "I know you do need green energy. *I* know that's where you're lacking, and *I* can see that because *I* have special skills."

Do you see what I'm saying? Light is perfect unto itself. It doesn't have to be qualified, divided. Do you see what I'm saying?

It doesn't have those kinds of requirements. The best healing that takes place is where the healer and the patient become the same energy. They find their connection, as you've already discovered, without all of the cerebral stuff that goes with it, without all that. The healer opens the door; the patient walks through. And the patient isn't threatened by the healer or intimidated by the healer, or isn't thinking that they are not good enough to walk through the door that the healer has opened.

The healer *is*. And being in the "is" state makes it perfectly accessible for the person who's being healed to walk through the door. It's more attractive for that person. It's easier for them to walk through, because they are not as intimidated by someone having more knowledge than they have. They are on the same level.

So, when you take all of that out of the equation, it's like taking rocks out of a flume. Water has to flow in all kinds of different ways until it hits the sea. Take all those rocks out and it flows.

The construct of reconnecting your life has to be established. Just reconnect your life through consciousness, daily actions, and thoughts. It begins by understanding that all of the greatness, all of the power, all of the joy that you could ever have, exists in this moment, and it's accessible this second. And leading people to that consciousness, that it is *now*. You do not have to delay gratification. You do not have to delay.

I will work very hard, and then in five years I will experience joy. No! It's all there *now*. We all came fully packaged. We just have to rediscover it. It's all here. It's not "there" anywhere. It's all here. It's all we need. Open those doors. Walk through them. Walk through them. It's here now.

We're here to understand compassion. We're here to open our lives to others, to be selfless in that endeavor. That's why we're here, to understand and recognize that we are all one, and that we rejoice in that understanding.

I'm going to leave you with that thought.

AFTERWORD

Marching Orders from Solomon

A NOTE FROM ERIC AND FRED: As this book comes to a close, we thought we'd share a bit about the approach that was taken in putting our conversations with Solomon into book form. Upon getting permission from Solomon to do so, we asked him for insight and direction on how to best convey this material. The following is a culling of the directions he communicated to us regarding these writings. We hope we have met this challenge. This process has been of great benefit to us, and we hope that it helps you on your journey.

There is knowledge, and then there's *access* to the knowledge. We, all of us, could certainly fill pages with very profound writing. But is it accessible? Does it reach into anyone's heart? That's where that message has got to start. With compassion. With clear compassion. Then you'll find that the book will write itself. It's there. But you can't force it; you can't drive it. You have to allow it to appear. And that takes trust in your ability. It takes trust. Confidence and trust.

I think the message of your book, if you intend to go forward with this, is clearing the way to a more fulfilling life. Creating the path for it.

In order to communicate this to a larger populace, you need to first evaluate the mission of that in terms of what you want to accomplish. It has to be very, very, very specific. It has to have a real, clear focus for you, and then you have to support that focus.

We want you to understand that there is a rhythm that will benefit your further endeavors in your quest to communicate. We know that you have much that you are trying to accomplish. You only need to be simple in your approach. You mustn't confuse your audience. We will find a way for you to express these concepts, but they have to be accessible, and you needn't carry them in a way that isn't decipherable to your existence out here. You really should start very, very simply, as if talking as a person in a room to another person. It should be very personal. *Very*—as if they are the only one in the world. That way they can absorb it if they feel the love through it.

So, when you approach this material, you need to make it very intimate. As if they are the only one who is understanding this. It's a question of creating trust. No one accepts a message if there's any kind of energy around it that they are questioning. That takes them out of the experience. So, from the very beginning, you must deal with them very one-on-one.

What we need to do in the opening of this work is to establish trust. Not from a viewpoint of *Well, this is being communicated from the other side* . . . but life-to-life. Because, in essence, this energy that is going to be communicated, this story that will be communicated, is already in their lives, and they have to trust it before that communication is connected to—this force to their force. If they distrust it at any level, it will never be absorbed, and it will not be accepted. We build our relationships on trust, and the moment that is forfeited, you can never regain that trust.

It's crucial in approaching this material that there is care and love on every page of whatever you write, and it's about nurturing and caring for the individual, the one person you are writing this book for.

Not for the masses. Not for the general "we" out there or the general "you." In your concept, it's as if you're writing it for one friend of yours. Just one. And if it has that kind of heart-to-heart communication, readers will relish the trust that they find from it and will then be able to absorb it. That's the only way it will work. The foundation of trust has to exist first if it's to be heard.

I want you to be all that you can be.

★ ◇ ★

EPILOGUE FROM FREDERICK

We are one and we are one.

— SOLOMON

S o now we have come to the end of the book, and hopefully a new beginning for you who have taken the time to read these pages.

I must tell you that I was extremely apprehensive about releasing this material into the world. But eventually I was won over by Eric's Pearly Gates argument and relented, after considerable thought. I came to believe, as pointed out in Eric's argument, that it is far better to err on the side of reaching out rather than not reaching out at all.

And that seems to be the primary message that Solomon espouses. In taking in this material in the exact same manner as you have (since I never remember any of the sessions after they are over), I come away with the visceral understanding that our growth is in our interaction . . . not our isolation. With every technological innovation that is introduced to allow us to contact one another more easily, there seems to be less real communication occurring. And the urgency with which Solomon addresses this only underscores the case for reaching out—whether it is as a healer or as one human being holding the candle to light the way for another.

Also, as Solomon reminds us, the intentional harm we do to one another is ultimately an act of self-flagellation. Solomon so succinctly expresses this when he tells us that "we are one and we are one." I don't think it could be stated any more clearly. And that, for me, is what I am left with.

I want to thank you, the reader, who have made the choice to reach out in absorbing this material. My sincere wish is that you are left with more, and that it will serve you well.

— Frederick Ponzlov

EPILOGUE FROM ERIC

There is a logical reason for everything that is happening in this world, and beyond—and it all makes perfect sense.

— Lois Pearl (Eric's late mother)

Without the wisdom of Aaron and Solomon, I don't know that I would have had the necessary determination to have brought Reconnective Healing onto the planet. When I was lost, frightened, or confused, I came to Aaron and Solomon. When I needed insight, I came to Aaron and Solomon. Fred's patience in being the "telephone" through which I could speak with them was a godsend in that it gave me the courage to persevere through everything . . . the biggest obstacle being my own self-doubt. The philosophy of this work is not an "easy grasp" for everyone. There is a commitment to this work and bringing it through in its purity that comes from an unshakable inner knowingness that there is both a need and a purpose for this.

Solomon has shown me that there is a clear reason and purpose for everything, and that everything makes perfect sense once we allow ourselves to step back three feet to observe the larger picture. Solomon has shone the light when the tunnel seemed the darkest.

I feel that we are more than fortunate if we discover our life purpose. And, truly, more's the better if we have the courage to live it. For Solomon and Aaron, I cannot thank you enough for allowing me to see my life purpose, and giving me the courage to live it.

— Eric Pearl

ACKNOWLEDGMENTS

From Eric: Thanks to Evelyn Sztojanov and Ronen Levy, whose belief in me, Reconnective Healing, and *The Reconnection* is an invaluable gift in my life. And to John Altschul, whose friendship is a constant I can always count on.

From Fred: Thanks to Sheri Leigh Myers, Tulis McCall, and Grace Lehman. Through their encouragement, Solomon flourished.

And a special acknowledgment to Dianna Bensch, who was both an unwavering support and a guiding light through the process of putting this book together.

ABOUT THE AUTHORS

Dr. Eric Pearl walked away from one of the most successful chiropractic practices in Los Angeles when he and others started witnessing miraculous healings. Today he has become the preeminent authority and acknowledged visionary on a new level of healing and life evolution on this planet, and has committed himself to sharing the light and information of the Reconnective Healing process through extensive lectures and seminars about "The Reconnection." Dr. Pearl has appeared on countless television programs in the U.S. and around the world. He has also spoken by invitation at the United Nations and has presented to a full house at Madison Square Garden, and his seminars have been featured in various publications, including *The New York Times.*

Website: **www.TheReconnection.com**

Frederick Ponzlov is a produced screenwriter, acting teacher, and award-winning actor. A graduate of the University of Wisconsin–Milwaukee, he studied acting at the Neighborhood Playhouse in New York and then journeyed west to Los Angeles. There he pursued a screenwriting career, and his first outing, *Undertaking Betty,* starring Naomi Watts, Christopher Walken, Brenda Blethyn, and Alfred Molina, won a BAFTA Award. Frederick has taught acting for the last 30 years and continues to do so in Long Beach, California, where he currently resides. The entity of Solomon has been with him most of his life, and after years of silence, this book marks his public debut.

Website: **www.fredponzlov.com**

Hay House Titles of Related Interest

YOU CAN HEAL YOUR LIFE, the movie, starring Louise Hay & Friends
(available as a 1-DVD program, an expanded 2-DVD set,
and an online streaming video)
Learn more at **www.hayhouse.com/louise-movie**

THE SHIFT, the movie,
starring Dr. Wayne W. Dyer
(available as a 1-DVD program, an expanded 2-DVD set,
and an online streaming video)
Learn more at **www.hayhouse.com/the-shift-movie**

✴

ASK AND IT IS GIVEN: Learning to Manifest Your Desires,
by Esther and Jerry Hicks (The Teachings of Abraham®)

THE HEART OF THE MATTER:
A Simple Guide to Discovering Gifts in Strange Wrapping Paper,
by Dr. Darren R. Weissman and Cate Montana, M.A.

MIND OVER MEDICINE: Scientific Proof That You Can Heal Yourself,
by Lissa Rankin, M.D.

SOUL LESSONS AND SOUL PURPOSE:
A Channeled Guide to Why You Are Here, by Sonia Choquette

THROUGH THE EYES OF ANOTHER: A Medium's Guide to Creating Heaven
on Earth by Encountering Your Life Review Now, by Karen Noe

TRANSCENDENTAL MEDITATION: The Essential Teachings of Maharishi
Mahesh Yogi: The Classic Text Revised and Updated, by Jack Forem

All of the above are available at your local bookstore,
or may be ordered by contacting Hay House (see next page).

✴

We hope you enjoyed this Hay House book. If you'd like to receive our online catalog featuring additional information on Hay House books and products, or if you'd like to find out more about the Hay Foundation, please contact:

Hay House, Inc., P.O. Box 5100, Carlsbad, CA 92018-5100
(760) 431-7695 or (800) 654-5126
(760) 431-6948 (fax) or (800) 650-5115 (fax)
www.hayhouse.com® • www.hayfoundation.org

———

Published in Australia by: Hay House Australia Pty. Ltd.,
18/36 Ralph St., Alexandria NSW 2015
Phone: 612-9669-4299 • *Fax:* 612-9669-4144
www.hayhouse.com.au

Published in the United Kingdom by: Hay House UK, Ltd.,
The Sixth Floor, Watson House, 54 Baker Street, London W1U 7BU
Phone: +44 (0)20 3927 7290 • *Fax:* +44 (0)20 3927 7291
www.hayhouse.co.uk

Published in India by: Hay House Publishers India,
Muskaan Complex, Plot No. 3, B-2, Vasant Kunj, New Delhi 110 070
Phone: 91-11-4176-1620 • *Fax:* 91-11-4176-1630
www.hayhouse.co.in

———

Access New Knowledge.
Anytime. Anywhere.

Learn and evolve at your own pace
with the world's leading experts.

www.hayhouseU.com

Listen. Learn. Transform.

Embrace your most sacred life with unlimited Hay House audios!

Live more consciously, strengthen your relationship with the Divine, and cultivate inner peace with world-renowned authors and teachers—all in the palm of your hand. With the *Hay House Unlimited* Audio app, you can learn and grow in a way that fits your lifestyle . . . and your daily schedule.

With your membership, you can:

- Tap into the power of your mind and heart, dive deep into your soul, rise above fear, and draw closer to Spirit.

- Explore thousands of audiobooks, meditations, immersive learning programs, podcasts, and more.

- Access exclusive audios you won't find anywhere else.

- Experience completely unlimited listening. No credits. No limits. No kidding.

Try for FREE!

Visit **hayhouse.com/free-trial** to start your free trial and get one step closer to living your best life.

Printed in the United States
by Baker & Taylor Publisher Services